Appalachian Folks

Eilleen Gardner Galer

Mabry Mill

Author:	Eilleen Gardner Galer
Designers:	Anne Pace
	Lou Chap
Cover Illustration:	Anne Pace
Publisher & Editor:	H. Donald Kroitzsh
Assistant Editor:	Barbara Ritchotte

Copyright © 1997 by Eilleen Gardner Galer. All rights reserved. No part of this publication may be reproduced, stored in a retrieval system or transmitted, in any form, or by any means, electronic, mechanical, recorded, photocopied, or otherwise, without the prior written permission of the copyright owners, except by a reviewer who may quote brief passages in a review. For information or orders contact Five Corners Publications, Ltd., HCR 70, Box 2, Plymouth, Vermont 05056, USA. Phone—802-672-3868

Printed in Canada.

Published by:
Five Corners Publications, Ltd.
HCR 70, Box 2
Plymouth, Vermont 05056—USA

Appalachian Folks
ISBN: 1-886699-06-2

Down ~~by~~ *in* the Old Mill Stream
In the days when Eilleen Galer was collecting the scenes now vanished

Appalachian Folks

Contents

Uncle Watt and the Telephone 1

Can You Hear Me, Zeke? 5

Belle 9

Titia Trail 17

About the Author 105

Uncle Watt and the Telephone

You know, it's funny when you stop and think about it, how some little something will have big consequences. It can change a person's whole life. Some little happenin', of no importance really, but just the way it strikes somebody else, it can be your ruination.

We had the first telephone in the town. Did I ever tell you the story of Uncle Watt and the telephone? You'll have to hear it. It's a good one.

Uncle Watt was a Baird, and Mother was a Baird. And the Keenes and the Bairds were always on opposite sides, in spite of the fact that Father married one. Uncle Watt voted opposite my father in elections. And so when they were trying to get the telephone in, they called on different ones. My father was one of the sponsors of it. But when they went up to see Uncle Watt he would have nothing to do with it. No, sir, he wasn't gonna have his house burnt down!

Well, after we had ours installed, there were all kinds of stories going the rounds about us and the telephone. Aunt Miry, who was a Free Will Baptist, came up and delivered a long lecture to Mother about our sinful ways. It just wasn't meant for man to talk over wires. Only God could talk through the air. And she predicted all kinds of dire trouble for us. Then, everybody heard about how we had been carefully instructed to disconnect it whenever a storm was coming up. And there was a story about how the wires killed every bird that lit on them. So there was much ado about killing the birds. Bill Tatum and I used to walk under the wires hunting the dead birds.

Then one day my father and mother went up to Grandfather's to see Uncle Henry. He was in the last stages of consumption, and they didn't expect him to live long. I stayed home to look after my sister. She was only a baby then.

We kids had been told not to fool with the phone, to let it alone. It wasn't a plaything. It was for more experienced hands to use. But sometimes when I was home alone I'd get me a stool and stand up and listen to see if anybody was talking. You knew when somebody was on the line because the phone would ring. And some of the things I heard over that line! They'd make stories worth telling too.

But this day I was home taking care of my sister I looked out and saw Uncle Watt coming up the walk with half a dozen men strung out behind him. I wondered what in the world Uncle Watt wanted. When he got to the door, he says, "Ernie, is Jim at home?" I could tell he was awful worried about something.

I says, "No, Uncle Watt. Him and Mother went up to Grandpap's. Uncle Henry's sick, and they don't think he'll live long."

I found out later what had happened, by piecing various stories together. Uncle Watt hauled timber. And he had sent a load over to town by James, his son. And he had forgot to tell James to fetch back a bolt he needed. So he was grouching about it down in the store when somebody said, "Jess Keenes has got a fome, Watt. Whyn't you go up and call up Dan Buchanan?" They knew Uncle Watt was scared to death of the phone. So another one joined it, "You hain't afeered of hit, air ye?" And they kep' needlin' Uncle Watt. "Why, anybody as back'ards and slow as you ort to be a-ridin' in a pole sled. Hit's a wonder you'd git on a mule, fer he mought throw you."

1

Well, they kept on, and after a while Uncle Watt just couldn't take it. So he commenced to boast: "No, I hain't afeerd of that contrapshun. Reckon I *will* call up Dan."

He figured, of course, that my father would make the call for him. And he didn't suppose the whole gang would go with him. But that's just what they did. They locked up the store, and the whole bunch walked the half a mile up right at this heels. And then, not to find my father home...

Uncle Watt took out his handkerchief and mopped his forehead. "Kin you use that thing, Boy?" he says to me.

I was just old enough to sense the glamour of the situation. "I know how to use it," I told him. "But Father said us kids should let it alone until we understood more about the mysteries of it." And, as if that wasn't enough, I added, "You know when there's lightning in the air, it cracks in the phone."

Uncle Watt swallowed on his Adam's apple. Then one of the crowd said, "Air you aimin', Watt, to make a boy do what you're afeerd to do?"

Uncle Watt looked at the phone. Then he went outside and looked as far as he could see along the wire. And he scanned the skies for signs of a storm. Then he came in and he says to me, "How do you work it, Boy?"

I was excited, and I spieled off what I had heard. "You hold the receiver to your ear and talk into the transmitter," I told him.

But the old man didn't get it. "How's that again?"

And I reeled it off as fast as before.

So he says, "Can you git Dan Buchanan fer me?"

I says, "You just ring a long and a short." And I climbed up on a stool and rung up Dan for him. When I heard the short ring back that showed that the party was on the line, I said, "Go ahead and talk, Uncle Watt. He's on the line."

Uncle Watt grabbed the receiver, but he'd forgotten my instructions. He put his ear to the mouthpiece and held the receiver away from him at arm's length, peering into it like it was a little peephole. "HELLO, DAN!" he yells. They always shouted as loud as they could in those days. "HELLO, DAN!"

I says, "No, not that way, Uncle Watt. You got it wrong. You talk through here, and put the receiver to your ear." I finally got him straightened out. But in changing around, he got the cord wrapped around his neck. By the time he got the receiver up to his ear, the static had commenced. He shouted, "My God, the LIGHTIN'S COMMENCED!" He yanked the receiver away from his ear, and as he did that, the cord tightened around his throat.

Well, I had to get him untangled. All this time you could hear, "Hello? Hello?" in the phone. So Uncle Watt says, "Dan? This here's Watt."

And Dan said, "Yeh, Watt. What can I do fer you?"

Uncle Watt says to me, "By God, the old skunk heard me!"

And Dan says, kinda mad, "What's that you say, Watt?"

At that Uncle Watt got flustered. He didn't know Dan could hear him. So he tried to cover up. He swallowed and wet his lips. He says, "That no-count son of mine, that skunk Jim, he's on his way over to yore place, Dan, and I want you to send me a bolt by him."

And Dan says, "What size bolt, Watt?"

Uncle Watt says, "'Bout that long." And he dropped the receiver to measure up his arm. The receiver struck against the wall and was broken.

Uncle Watt never lived it down. About that time he was courting a well-to-do widow woman that lived across the valley. Everybody said he was plum gone on her. But seems like she couldn't make up her mind. She told Mother that she liked Watt well enough, but she couldn't stand the way he wore his hat. The evening would come when she was about to say, "Yes"; then Watt would jam on his old hat, and that changed everything.

Well, the affair of the phone got talked around, and that cooked Uncle Watt's goose. Next thing we heard, she had jilted Uncle Watt for a likely feller who'd been hangin' around...just in case.

After that, Uncle Watt was a beat old man. He pined away. And it wasn't long till somebody found him dead.

They buried him in a pauper's grave.

The sign reads, "Omar Khayyam Pottery - Visitors Always Welcome"
This and Jugtown give some idea of the facilities that produced handsome pottery

O. L. Bachelder, artist/potter, Omar Khayyam Pottery, Candler, NC

Can You Hear Me, Zeke?

He couldn't sit still, the little old man up front in the bus beside the stout lady. As soon as we stopped at the landslide completely blocking the road, he began to fidget. When the driver stepped off to gauge the situation, closing the door behind him, the old man tried to keep calm by studying the faces of nearby passengers, one by one. But all the while, his foot kept tapping impatiently amongst the peanut hulls on the floor. And every few minutes he stretched his scrawny neck to observe any progress made by the road crew clearing the highway.

Twice he pulled his big, battered watch by its braided leather strap from the bib pocket of his overalls. The second time he stared at it, held it to his ear, shook it vigorously, then listened again. Turning to the stout lady, he said politely,

"Scuse me, ma'am. Have you the time?"

Learning that it was even later then he thought, he scowled and shook his head fretfully. With great care he set and wound his ancient turnip, grumbling meanwhile:

"Foolin' round this-a-way we cain't help but be in the dark a-glittin' thar. If'n that slow poke of a driver'd jest kep' on time like he ort, we'd a-done hit the road ahead of the slide. But here we set! An' I tol' my sweetie to meet me down at the stop. I don't want the dark to ketch her all by her lone."

Listening to his complaint the stout lady measured him with a glance that took in his whole person from the crown of his old slouch hat right down his faded overalls to the soles of his scuffed brogans. Her look plainly said, "Probably some dumb country girl thinks he's wonderful." And she tried to settle him with the vague promise that they would soon be on their way.

The old man scarcely noticed her. "Reckon I hadn't orter gone to Hester Ann's today," he muttered. Then plaintively he asked, "But how could I tell the storm was a-goin' to wash the mount'n down?"

Peering ahead once more at the heap of earth and rock still to be shoveled away, he fumed, "Doggone it! Seem like the bigger the hurry, the more thengs they is to hender. I don't want to keep my sweetie a-waitin' fer me in the dark."

At that moment someone toward the rear of the bus began to strum a banjo. The old man screwed around to get a good look at the player. His pale watery eyes lit up, his thin lips curved into a smile. Then, as a lively tune accompanying a nasal voice drifted down the aisle, he leaned back, folded his horny hands against his stomach, and listened with rapt attention.

When presently the musician laid aside his instrument, the old man heaved a deep sigh.

"Sounds plumb sweet to these ol' ears, lemme tell yuh now," he confided to the stout lady. "My ol' mammy uster seng them songs. An' I'd pick the banjer. But I hain't picked a tune in twenty year, I reckon." He snapped his fingers. "Come to think of hit, my ol' banjer still hangs up in the attic. I'll jest hafter git hit down." Again he sighed. "I keep a-thinkin' of all the thengs I wanter do. Don't reckon I'll git 'em all done though, my time bein' kindly short. From here on out."

5

The stout lady inclined her head and regarded him with lips pursed and eyebrows raised, favoring him with her attention.

Settling himself more comfortably, he continued sociably. "I don't reckon, ma'am, most folks stops to think how lonesome a feller can git when he's all shet up inside hisself and can't hear nothin' atall. Course they's a heap of things you don't wanter hear. But then they's a-plenty you do. You set and watch folks's mouths a-workin' and you watch 'em laugh. But the joke's plumb lost on you. And you cain't hear the banjer ner the guitar. All you got to pleasure yoreself air old moldy ricollections. And tain't long afore you git mighty tared of jest yore own comp'ny. Seem like folks cain't take the time ner trouble to be aller a-hollerin' at ye, and if'n they's to wanter whisper some leetle sweet somepin, they'd not keer about a-yellin' hit to all creation. And when strangers speaks perlite, and you don't answer nary word back, they figger you're jest stoopid." He nodded his head emphatically. "I know all about hit. Yes, ma'am."

He thought a moment, his forefinger across his lips. "Still," he went on, "Hit had kinder slipped my mind all I's a-missin' ontil I got me one of these here contrapshuns what makes a feller hear purty good even if he's deef as a post, like me."

Proudly he twisted around to show her the hearing aid in his right ear. "This hyer's a wonderful contraption, you know hit? Why, I can even hear the crickets a-chirpin' by me upper door! Hit's somep'n fine early of a mornin' to hear the birds a-sengin'. I hain't had the thing not three good days yet, and I've purt nigh wore hit out jest a-listenin'. I listen to the pigs a-gruntin', and a peckerwood rat-a-tattin' in a tree, and my old dog in the woods clost by a-tellin' me he's found a possum.

"An' this mornin' I tuk the notion to go over and visit my wife's sister, Hester Ann. That's whur I've been. I never heerd my wife's nat'ral voice, fer her and me got hitched atter I turned deef. She was a mighty fine woman, my wife was. I buried her three years, two months and ten days ago tomorrer. But her and her sister, Hester Ann, they was borned twins. Sense they looked alike, I figgered they'd talk alike. So I goes up to Hester Ann a-bendin' over the wash pot and I calls her name. She hollers back at me. I drawed myself up and give 'er a leetle wave of my han', puttin' on airs, and I says, 'Jest a minute, sister'," I says, "'don't be a-hollerin' at me that-a-way.'" And her eyes purt nigh popped out'n her head.

"So then I showed her my contrapshun. And she'as tickled as me. Hester Ann's a great talker, and she never shet her mouth all afternoon. Between givin' me the dirt on all the scan'lous doin's of folks we both knowed, she jawed that shiftless old man of her'n. An' I kep' a-sayin' to myself, "That thar's my woman a-talkin'."

"But wait till I tell you the fust thing I done when I got my contrapshun. I wouldn't even wear hit home the day I bought hit, fer I'd made up my mind that the fust thing I wanted to hear was my gal's sweet voice. She's the purtiest flower ever bloomed out. She's got ha'r the color of corn tossels, and sich purty blue eyes. Her and me fell in love with one another right atter my wife died, and I's a-pinin' all my lonesome.

"So then she says, 'Can you hear me, Zeke?'"

"Them was her very fust words. I almost busted out a-cryin'. I jest nods my head."

"So then she says to me, bashful-like, 'Do you love me, Zeke? Hug my neck.'"

"So then I tuk 'er on my lap—there was the mere breath of a pause—fer she ain't but ten year old." He gave the stout lady an innocent smile. "She's my neighbor's child, but I love 'er jest like she's my own. She's been a heap of comfort to me. "So we hugged one another. And I says, "'Whose gal are you?' And she says, 'Zeke's gal'.

"So then she slips down to run home, fer she's a-gonna be in a play at the school and she had to larn her part.

"An' that's why I've bin in sich a swivvet to git along home afore dark. She'll be a-waitin' fer me thar at the turn of the road whur the bus stops... an' a-watchin' fer me with them purty blue eyes...She'll grab a-holt of my hand an' go skippin' along aside of me, a-talkin' about how she was a wicked witch in the play."

The bus driver returned to announce there would probably be another hour's delay.

The old man jumped up. "Doggone if'n I'm a-goin' to set here all night long, rock slide or not. I'll jest hoof it." He doffed his shapeless hat. "Good day, ma'am. Please to me ye. But I jest cain't keep my gal disapp'inted."

Appalachian Folks

Belle Harwood

Belle

In town (fifty years ago), with only news stories to form their judgment, people had the impression that Helton's Cove was one of the more unsavory localities in the mountains. Heltons were notorious for troubles amongst themselves, which had given their wild, rugged homeplace a bad name.

Not distant as the crow flies, but so walled around by towering peaks as to be virtually inaccessible, the high cove had years ago offered a haven sufficiently remote to suit Big Matt Helton when he swapped his proud pioneer family for his love, the beautiful brown girl. They made a matched pair, equals in tough-minded independence, indifferent to the stigma of misalliance for themselves and their descendants. And they sought the wilderness, there to make their own world together. In isolation their family grew. Now, several generations later, the cove's rock-ribbed barriers confined a race of dark-skinned people different and disesteemed whose misdeeds ran something like a continued story.

As the cove crowded up there was feuding among them. And violence. By night a kinsman was waylaid and clubbed into insensibility. Bad feeling between an older leader and a young upstart came to a head over a bear and bear dogs, with a senseless killing.

Ominous news being all we ever heard of the Helton's, they shaped up in our minds as a clan of ill-tempered individuals mad at the world and "jest spilin' fer a fight." And their private hills, looming up northeasterly, seemed a sinister, forbidding region wisely shunned.

But out in the country, enjoying the cool evening and the plaint of mountain music on Wagner's porch beside the Woody Branch, I discovered a different attitude toward the Heltons.

"The way you admire them old-timey tunes," Sam said when his wife laid aside the guitar, "you'd orta hear fiddlin' Bart Helton. I'm a-tellin' you, Bart's fiddlin' would put heart in a holler stump." He eased his back against the porch post and brought his left brogan up beside its mate on the stepstone. "We mought could get him to make music—"

"Not one of the Heltons of Helton's Cove?" I thought he was stringing me.

"Well, yes'm," he admitted, trying to conceal his amusement by studying his fingers laced together. "Only Bart he don't live right in the cove proper. He's one of 'em that's got scrounged down the branch a piece. Three or four whoppin ginerations cain't *all* find foot room in one little holler. And Helton's ain't noways shy on younguns. There's a passel of boys, and some real pretty gals, when young."

Lizzie said, "Oh, the young folk are mostly all fine lookin' stock, them I've seen. You can easy tell 'em. They've got eyes dark as chinkypins and mostly they're black headed as a crow."

"Back in my courtin' days," Sam continued, "a sister of Bart's named Belle was pretty as a rose just bloomed out. I could've easy took a fancy to her." His teasing glance swept over his stout placid wife.

She gave him no notice. "Oh, I reckon she could've had any feller in the settlemint. She could, and she couldn't, the way things was. I only ever seen her once. She was slim as a willer switch, with them dark eyes and a plait of black hair thick as your arm. She come down to the school house. But the younguns stared her down. And they turned their backs on her. She never come back. One of the gals said, 'We'd orta throw it up to her, what her old granmaw was.' I said, 'No, now, that ain't right and Christian. She cain't help what her granmaw was'."

"But they're quare," Sam put it. "You'd orta hear 'em talk. I reckon they talk English, but even I cain't understand 'em all times. And the women-folks are more antic than the men."

"Probably because they don't see many people," I suggested.

"Oh, I reckon strangers up their way don't exactly cumber the road," he agreed dryly. "That's wild, rough country up that-a-way—the people and the land."

His candor only strengthened my suspicions that Helton's Cove was hardly the healthiest place to go questing for old-time "song ballets." But he hastened to reassure me.

"Oh, they'll treat *you* right. It's among themselves they run wrong. The pleasantest place in the world to live is where you don't know nobody. When you've got kinfolks all up and down the branch, they think up everything they can to tell on you. They go way back and tell things so old you don't know what they're a-talkin' about."

I still doubted. But Sam ought to know. He was born and raised on the spring branch that babbled past his door, close enough for some neighborly knowledge of the Heltons.

Lizzie doubted that they could be persuaded to play for a stranger. "Even when I'm around," she said, "and they know me, they're too shy to start a tune. They just set with their backs to me."

But Sam was stubborn. "Well, there cain't be no harm in askin'. I'll put it to Bart the next time I ketch 'im down at the store."

About a month later Lizzie sent word for me to come on out. And Sam met me at their door, triumphant. "I got the promise of it!" His ruddy face beamed. "We'll head for Bart's in the mornin'. He'll be on the lookout for us."

Accordingly, church time Sunday morning found us climbing into the high mountains. The weather was crisply fair, with fleecy clouds lazily drifting overhead, their shadows shifting on the green slopes below.

Upon a high saddle we came to Bart's place, looking away to distant smoke-blue peaks, and down into the deep valley upon cabins in their patchwork of small fields. But his dooryard was totally bare of greenery, and in a wallow of black ooze a couple of hogs snuffed and grunted.

Sam, following the path in, hollered the house.

A plump woman with a flock of gaping children appeared in the shadow of the doorway. Bart, she said, had gone up the road to his sister's. She reckoned he intended to make music. He took his fiddle with him.

Sam was baffled. But not for long. Clearly, if we would hear music, we must push on higher toward the more remote haunts of the Heltons. And having come this far, he was not to be denied.

The road ahead was steep and narrow and rough. We decided to walk. Granpaw Wagner, along for the ride, was left in my car.

Was this the way, years ago, that Big Matt Helton and his brown-skinned woman had climbed skyward toward their private heaven? He, the stalwart son of a proud pioneer family, who had acquired some book-learning to equip him for a bright future; she a woman of mixed-blood so beautiful in his eyes that he turned deaf ears to whisperings about her origin, so desirable that he weighed as nothing the stigma of misalliance for himself and his children and his children's children.

He sold his land, so the story goes, loaded his house-plunder on a wagon hitched to mules, and turned his back on his birthright. With the brown beauty by his side, he set out in search of a retreat in the wilderness where he and she could make their own world. And they found to their liking the high, shut-in cove with good soil and sweet water.

Perhaps just here where the road levels off before the next upward climb, the pair halted to let the mules blow. And looking back, deep into the heart of the populous valley, down the chimneys of neighbors and kin whose disdain had driven them to flight, they felt no regrets or misgivings; else now there would be no clan several generations strong.

As we followed the loopings of the old road, the slopes on either hand grew so steep that the land stood almost on end and the rail fences climbed skyward like ladders, but no house was to be seen. Toiling up the breast of the mountain, I thought, "They were no weaklings, that pair!" And the brown girl who spent her youth and beauty in solitude: once there, did she ever leave?

Her numerous brood grew up unlettered and wild as woods creatures. In time the cold shoulder of their near neighbors cut them to the quick. They nursed hurt and resentfulness. Their bitterness was shared by those who cast their lot with them. Living conditions grew more and more difficult, forcing them to ventures outside the law. And a big dish of trouble was what they got, according to Sam.

We took a short-cut through a ribbed pasture broken by outcroppings of rock and clumps of horsemint in flower. Sam opined that Bart must have preceded us by only a breath of time, for the draw-bars were still down.

Soon we came again to the rutted road, now following the sharp backbone of the ridge and offering spectacular views. Then woods closed in about us. So far the road had been deserted.

But now, with startling suddenness, we met two young men with their dark-eyed girls, walking arm in arm. They were good-looking, all of them.

Sam greeted them with a grave, "Howdy," and a wave of his hand, to which the lads responded politely.

Empty again, the road wound away beyond leafy turns, dappled with sunlight and shadow, dipping to the run-off from a spring cupped under the hillside. Around a bend we came at last upon a house. But it was shut and silent, guarded by a pair of solemn hound dogs that appeared noiselessly underneath the porch and stood side by side, eyeing us.

Sam hollered the house, but there was no answer. I wondered whether these people had *just* left, alerted by the strolling couples. Perhaps it was only over-active imagination, but I had a creepy feeling that eyes were spying upon us. A friend had described his experience, telling one of his mountain stories: "You go into these coves," he said, "and they're silent as a tomb. The cabins are closed. Everybody has disappeared. But you feel their presence, peering out at you from the laurel."

Sam was undaunted. "Well," he said, "the road ain't give out yet. We'll just keep on till we come to the next house. Somebody's bound to live up this here way."

We trudged on, Sam busy figuring, trying to overtake the fugitive Bart. "His sister's," she said. "That could be Belle or Janie or t'other'n. But it don't differ. I don't rightly know where airy one of 'em lives." He chuckled. "Sposin' it's Belle. I ain't seen her in Lord knows how many years."

Snaking through the quiet woods for another quarter of a mile or so, the road finally gave out in a clearing where some lumbering had been going on. There, side by side, stood a small box house, planked up and down, and a larger, much older, chinked and daubed cabin. The doors were tight shut.

"Well, now," Sam said aside, "this here mought be Bart's sister's little old dirt-dauber's nest."

There seemed to be nobody about. But the faintest wisp of smoke hovered over the nearer chimney.

Suddenly, out back, a women rabbited off into the woods. Quickly she disappeared in the underbrush.

We walked on around to the upper doors, one of which stood ajar, and there we caught unawares a youngish women just crossing the yard.

In his politest voice Sam inquired whether Bart Helton was at home.

She froze in her tracks. But she managed to answer in a stifled voice, "I hain't seed 'im," her face averted.

As we continued to approach, she retreated toward the house, keeping her eyes fixed on the ground, hanging her head in painful timidity.

Sam kept repeating his inquiries about Bart, moving nearer all the while, and she kept answering that she hadn't seen him, withdrawing until he stood before the open door and she was inside behind it. Only the cookstove was visible, and a pine table with a split-bottomed chair standing before a short wall papered with newspapers where dishcloths and a tin dishpan hung on nails.

Sam talked on, to the blank doorway. The girl edged away along the wall from the door corner until finally she reached the chair where she sat down with her back to him. He persisted:

"And you say Bart ain't here? I cain't understand it. Why, just last Wednesday he promised to make music, and here we are."

She drawled, "I hain't seed 'im," venturing a slantwise glance in his direction.

Meanwhile, the curiosity of the woman hiding in the bushes got the best of her, and she commenced creeping cautiously back toward the house. When she came in sight on the leafy trail, Sam turned his attention to her, still inquiring about the missing Bart.

She froze in her tracks exactly as had the younger woman, and stood silently studying us, but ready to bolt back into the woods. After a bit, Sam's friendly voice reassured her. She ventured a few steps nearer, growing bolder, staring into our faces, but never answering, until she stood on the edge of the dooryard. Then she began to giggle.

She was stooping tall and spare. In repose her face was a mask of tragedy; eyes sunken and sorrowful, her mouth drooping at the corners. She had bad teeth. Her graying hair had been hacked off into ragged bangs. She wore an ill-fitting cotton jacket, a dun-colored homespun skirt sagging behind, and a man's heavy brogans.

Sam good-naturedly repeated his queries as to the whereabouts of the elusive Bart.

Her only response was uncontrollable giggling. She squatted in the path, drawing a tall dahlia in front of her, trying to hide her painful embarrassment. Nervously she stood up, giggling. At last she managed to speak. "Wal, I'll tell yuh, friend," she drawled, "Bart an' the folks air all gone a-viewin'. They got a soon start this mornin' fer Hickses Knob."

"Hickses Knob! Sam exclaimed. "Why, that's twenty miles. Did they aim to be gone all day?"

His astonishment struck her as very funny. She had another giggling fit. When she could control herself she said, "Wal, I'll tell yuh, friend, they tuk their denner with 'em." She fidgeted, giggling, stooping among the dahlias, then standing up. Finally she added a little helplessly, "They air powerful to view."

Sam explained once more that Bart had promised to make music for his friend from town, and only last Wednesday had invited us up today.

She listened, absently plucking the leaves from a tall dahlia. The situation tickled her. "I bet a dollar my folks is hid," she said, looking wise. "They're wild as b'ars."

Refusing to be discouraged, Sam began on her. "You Bart's sister?"

She nodded.

"Are you Belle Helton?"

She nodded again.

"Then I know you play. Won't you save this here nice lady from disapp'intment by making some real old-time music?"

She giggled and squirmed, fingering the pins on her jacket, not knowing where to look, again stooping and standing. But she stood her ground. "I'd feel so strange," she drawled.

"You shorely cain't let good folks go away disapp'inted," he coaxed. "City people cain't hear our kind of music every day."

"Wal, I'll tell yuh, friend, I wushed my suster was hyer." She turned her gaze vaguely up the trail. "She picks the banjer."

For a time this was her answer to all entreaty.

Sam's good-humored begging took on a note of weariness. He got very warm.

But just when importunity seemed futile, the woman's face suddenly sobered. She stood silent, studying the smooth-swept dooryard. Then without a word she moved like one in a trance across to the cabin door. She disappeared inside. We could hear her drawling voice:

"Them's the best friends ever I seed." There was the tuning of a violin. And she repeated, "Them's the best friends ever I seed."

Directly she emerged carrying an old violin all dressed up. A red satin bow graced the ebony tailpiece, and from the scroll dangled bright green streamers. She dragged forth a stumpy-legged hickory chair and sat down in the sunshine against the cabin wall. She laid the fiddle along her arm, resting her elbow in her lap. The bow she grasped almost a third the way along, three fingers above the stick, her thumb and little finger resting on the horsehair.

So she sawed away at old familiar tunes, her head thrown back, eyes closed, and a smile on her lips. There were dance tunes and favorite old hymns. Finishing each piece, she giggled self-consciously, then began another without urging.

As her confidence increased, she admitted that she picked the banjo. But it was shut up in the other house and she could not open the door. "Fer that's an ol' penetenchery lock," she explained, "an' I cain't pick hit."

"We'll hear it next time," Sam said cheerfully. The sun was past noon and we hadn't thought to bring our dinner. He shuffled his feet, about to start down the road. "Kind thanks fer them old tunes," he told her.

I thanked her for saving our day.

But she was not ready to have us leave. Spying the young women who, so far ignored, had ventured to the door, Belle said, "Come out hyer and meet the folks. This hyer's my gal, friends."

The daughter forced a weak smile, revealing dark teeth. She wore an over-large gigham dress and a man's heavy brogans. From behind her skirts she drew a blonde child of about eight who squinted in the sunlight. She was told to pick a posy for the lady. Dazed with wonder, hardly taking her eyes off me, she pulled the head of a crimson dahlia and offered it in a small hot hand.

Sam was saying, "So you're Belle."

She nodded. "That's me. My mother was a Helton and married a Helton, and I was a Helton and married a Helton." She giggled. "I reckon that makes me a full-blooded Helton."

"And you can fiddle a mighty fine tune," he told her, edging toward the road.

"Yo're mighty natcherel and good to me," she drawled. "I'm a country subject, but I do love to see strangers. An' I feel yore kindness to me."

I repeated Sam's compliment, feeling honored that she had so far overcome her timidity to save us from disappointment.

She followed us around the cabin, saying, "Wal, I declar', I hain't afeered of strangers. I've bin a widder women fer nigh onto fifteen year up hyer on this ol' lonesome mountain. But I hain't afeerd of strangers. I've traveled. I've bin to South Ca'lina in my husband's lifetime."

We moved away. But she tagged after, seeking to postpone the moment of parting with a gift of knotty apples she gathered up from under a couple of twisted old trees.

At last we must tear ourselves away. She laid her hand on my shoulder and said plaintively, "When you comin' back to see me?"

I could only answer that I didn't know; the way was difficult.

"Wal, don't make hit too long," she said. "I mought be dead."

We left her there watching us out of sight, her shoulders sagging, her face woebegone, all the loneliness and hunger of her soul plain to read. We waved. She waved back. Then the road turned and the leafy woods closed over her.

Belle Harwood with daughter and granddaughter

Cynthia Ann Elizabeth Creasman by her Snowball bush, Bent Creek Road

Titia Trail

Chapter I

he was the first white child born on Laurel Fork, far back in the wilds of the southern Appalachians. July the 23rd, it was. Way late of a night, with a storm commencing to mutter off in the distance, and only her pappy on hand.

"I come right smart afore my time," Aunt Titia said, reaching for her poking stick to rouse the fire. "You could kiver my face with the palm of yore hand. And they thought I'd not live."

But she stalled off the hovering angels. And now in her eighty-fifth year the doomsayers were again sure that her time was short.

Any such fool notion rubbed her patience sore. "I tell 'em I'm ready to go when my time comes, but I hain't in no hurry." She gave the simmering logs a couple of vicious jabs. Then sunniness broke through the shade of her annoyance. "Hit's a pyore marvel the things they is to see and do in this world. And twixt me and you, I hain't nowheres near through."

Indomitable as she was, my friend would likely finish out a century. She had it in mind. You can live as long as you want to, claimed other old timers. And her streak of contrariness hadn't wizened yet.

Weighing little more than one hundred pounds, withered and bent as a wind-runted tree, she still lived in the old log cabin raised by her parents on cleared land. And there she dearly hoped to end her days.

"I love my leetle hut," she said. "Me and hit's both old together."

Alone now eighteen years, ever since her old pappy died, she clung to her blessed singleness. So far, her independent spirit and proud self-reliance had kept her free. She still cut most of her own firewood and planted her crops.

"Bless yore life," she said. "I make me own rations, and I have as fine a time as ever you seed. Nobody to rare at me, nobody to quarrel with. I've got two clocks. One's too fast, t'other'n's too slow; so I eat and go to bed between 'em."

But of late the thread of her existence was becoming frazzled by aggravations. For hers was the universal struggle of aged persons, fighting for life, their liberty and the pursuit of happiness as their hearts desire.

Through good times and bad she had lived most every way, "on top of the pot and under hit", as the saying is, and she had always managed. But now old age troubles commenced to plague her. And the family kept faulting her for staying all alone up on her old lonesome mountain.

Hard times and worrisome folks she could handle. The Lord's will was something else. She who once cradled wheat and split logs, able as any man, still had the grit but not the strength. If she hoed corn too long, she got the weak trembles. And squatting down at the fireplace to tend her cooking, she might take a swimming in her head.

But she kept secrecy about her ailments, knowing full well that her kin needed only the triflingest excuse to move her down among the family. Dread of that lay rock-heavy in the back of her mind. For a chair in somebody else's chimney corner was the last thing she wanted in this world. The old ways suited her best. So why worry about no door neighbors in hollering distance, or that the old house might fall down and smash her to a poultice. All depending on who and when, she turned her deaf ear to their nag or she faced them down—"Long's I'm fit and able to move, I'll have my satisfaction right here in me own old house. Hit makes no diff'rence whur I set down, I hain't in nobody's way, they's nobody to mutter about hit. I can git up soon or git up late in my leetle log cabin."

And that was the size of it. For a while—

Cynthia Creasman's cabin, Bent Creek

Chapter II

My acquaintance with Aunt Titia came about through a chance meeting with one of her kin. Though I was a stranger just passing on the road, towards noon of a fair October day, I stopped at a cabin home and asked permission to watch the family making sorghum molasses. Tillie Trail, a large woman in neat flower print dress and fresh white apron, was skimming the green juice that boiled in a large flat pan on a lively fire. But a bearded elder standing nearby silently reached and took over while she crossed the yard to greet me.

The crispy Fall weather had lured me to considerable climbing already, and now, toiling up the long slope to her house, I was beginning to sag. I said, "I'm all tuckered out."

She chuckled, waved her hand toward a couple of chairs under an old apple tree, and gave me hearty welcome, "Well, sit a spell and rest your tucker."

Making molasses, simply put, means grinding the cane and boiling down the juice. "But there's more to it than that," Tillie said. "There's a kind of knack to makin' molasses. And it's a knack that ain't easy learned. You've got to have a feel fer when it's ready. You don't want it too thin, ner too thick. You have to know when it's just right."

Somebody called her to the house and I was left to watch. The monotonous work went on. Round and round plodded a big bay horse, leading himself by a halter rope tied to a pole revolving just ahead of him. A wispy woman in droopy straw hat and sagging brown sweater jammed stalk after stalk between the stone rollers of the cane mill. And steadily the green juice flowed into a barrel, strained through a sack. A lanky sunbrowned lad in patched overalls made himself useful carrying cane from a loaded sled to the mill and feeding the fire from a handy woodpile. The old gent never slackened his motions above the pan from which rose a mist of yellow steam. The boiling must go on however long it takes to turn eighty gallons of juice into about ten gallons of molasses. That usually means three to four hours, and the green scum must be constantly skimmed off. "After a while it turns a pretty gold-brown color," Tillie said. She glanced at the sky. "We planned to make two runs today, but I reckon we'll be in the dark on the second one. We'll have to work by lantern light and moonshine."

The sun, high overhead, shone down full and strong. The horse sneezed. You heard the jingle of his harness, and the happy sing-song of a fat brown hen scratching in the dirt near the barn. But the people worked on silently. It occurred to me that my presence might be a hindrance; so I invented an engagement.

"Now you come see us again," Tillie said cordially. "Come back when we ain't so busy." And she handed me a small jar of molasses. "I thought you might like a little taste with your pancakes."

Such graciousness warmed the heart of a stranger. And so began our enduring friendship. Tillie was a happy-hearted, capable woman whom nothing dismayed

19

seemingly; a person so genuinely kind that everybody loved her. When I drove out for a short visit, she dropped whatever she happened to be doing and welcomed me with open arms. "Bless you, I've been a-savin' my tongue to talk," she would say with a deep throaty chuckle.

It happened that both of us had a hobby of genealogy. Beyond her motherly joys in a numerous brood, she had long pleasured herself with a "mort" of handed down tales precisely remembered. To her mind, family affairs were a heap more interesting than any story, because book people are just make-believe, while the shadowy characters she cherished were once real live folks. Her folks. And while none of them ever made a big splash in history, still, tradition had it that the earliest Trail in this country accumulated large experience fighting the Indians and was a soldier on the American side in the Revolutionary War. Although his descendents never got much richer than the common lot, they lived upright and useful lives. And it made her feel proud that so many long dead survived in her memory.

Aunt Titia was first mentioned one sultry afternoon when we were sitting out in the dooryard to catch a little breeze because Tillie thought the vines on her porch were so smothersome. Also, from our spot of shade she could better keep an eye on her two youngest playing ridey-hossy with an old hickory chair down the path to the spring.

She spoke of Tim Trail, a great bear hunter in olden times when bears were plentiful almost as rabbits are today. And how his oldest girl Titia likely saved her pappy's life.

It happened along the fringes of one of those thickety places they call hells. A monstrous big bear, frenzied by the tormenting dogs, suddenly broke through the laurel from an unexpected quarter and grabbed hold of Uncle Tim, cuffing the gun from his hands. All he could do was wrestle with the bear while he tried to stick it with his knife. But the fighting was so close, and the footing risky, that the bear came near getting the best of him.

"Then here come little old Tish with her rifle-gun and she wilted the varmint."

Uncle Tim had more than one close call, of course. But in spite of the hardships and ever-present dangers in wild unsettled country, and three years war service besides, the worthy man lived his span to green old age.

Tillie's interest in her ancestors began during her girlhood. Those days, she told me, when the Trails had a reunion they put the young folks to studying who they were. Each family remembered back. Back even to their foreparents who came over from faraway England in a boat that took eighty-seven days to cross the ocean.

Three generations later Tim Trail moved westward through the Blue Ridge, to become the pioneer settler of the Laurel Fork section.

"Uncle Tim couldn't never take well to idleness," Tillie said, fanning with her wash-faded bonnet. "And he never let his family rest neither. That's why he was worth a little somethin' when it come time for him to die.

"But in the beginnin' him and Aunt Rindy was pore as Job's turkey. They come from Yancey county, and some places they had to cut their way. Just make a little trail. They was nine days on the road. And I've heard tell they carried ever'thing they owned in a split basket and a bag.

"How come that was, him and her deserted home. Aunt Rindy's paw was agin her marryin' so young, and her never noways strong. But, wouldn't you know, them two up and run off together.

"They come to the Laurel Fork section on account of talk he'd heard about gold in the creek branches, and garnets and suchlike that could be picked out of the mountain rocks. Well, they never found no gold in the creeks, ner garnets in the rocks. But they found peace. They liked the wild country. So they staked 'em out a homestead, grooved the cabin together, and settled down with the wolves and the rattlesnakes. There wasn't a stick of timber amiss on the place.

"Aunt Tish was the first little'n horn on Laurel Fork. And she still lives in the old house."

"Where is it?"

"The Trail cabin? Where is it? Oh, it's just along the side the road before you get anywhere..."

Tillie's attention was on the pair with their ridey-hossy. A dispute seemed to be heating up. But something amused the towheads. One chuckled. They both laughed. And their mother's watchfulness relaxed.

Before us the view gave a long eye-reach. Somewhere hidden away in the serene blue yonder was the Trail cabin.

"It's old as the hills, pret' near. And Aunt Tish, she's old too. She's all by herself now up there on her old lonesome mountain. But she won't move. You'd as easy uproot the big oak tree in her yard as her from the old homeplace. Sweet-talk her or argufy, it don't differ. She just says: 'I got wooden ears. I cain't hear a thing you say.'

Tillie loosened a sigh. "She's a little bitty old lady, but she's got spirit, Aunt Tish has. She always done just as she pleased, no matter what. And I reckon she always will. The kinfolks fret and nudge, fer it ain't fitten at her age to live way off where a body's got no door neighbors. But you cain't reason with her. Seem like so long as she's fit and able, she cain't rest easy nowhere but nested up there on the old place. That little old crooked back of her'n stiffens up and she says:

"I love my leetle hut. Me and hit's both old together."

Appalachian Folks

Cynthia Creasman, Bent Creek Road, Patching a quilt

Chapter III

I came upon it suddenly, in a loop of the road just emerging from a stretch through solitary woods. Downside the hill a little way, beyond a snake-rail fence and gentle grassy slope, was settled a quaint hewn log cabin over-shadowed by its venerable White Oak. On the porch sat an old lady. Evening sunshine kindled bright red patchwork in her lap.

Aunt Titia Trail. And as old Demon Hately would remark, "She'd fit into anybody's pitcher book."

My late start and dalliance along the way meant that I had to pass on by. But I waved to her. And she returned my greeting.

Down in the valley I came upon Pink Meaders' ruinous store building, patched over patches with weathered timbers and garish metal signs. Past the sagging screen door you entered a clutter of hardware, drygoods and groceries, and the pervading odors of cheese and fat back, coffee, tobacco and bucket candies. Hoes, rakes and shovels leaned against sacks and boxes; horse collars hung above bolts of cloth and spools of thread. The plentiful stock of snuff carried several brand names on drums large and small. A rusted potbelly stove, flanked by ample spit boxes, occupied center floor space. Its smoke pipe, supported by wires from above, extended the full length of the room before it disappeared through a side wall.

The storekeeper, a cripple with red hair and a gold front tooth, was up hanging flypaper curls on the ceiling. He backed down his ladder to sell me a pack of cigarettes.

I spoke of the old lady up the road.

He flashed a smile. "Oh, that's Granny Trail. A mighty fine woman."

Mention of her name "set the talk a-drappin," as Uncle Demon put it. A hatchet-faced individual slammed through the screen door just then, and she hutted in. "*Miss* Trail." She gave me a sly smirk. "Although she has a son."

Her presence deferred my sociability with the storekeeper. I picked up my change and left. But a week or so later I went back. Pink Meaders sat on the store porch, tilted back in his chair, studying the horizon. But he gave me a pleasant "Howdy". His appreciation of the old grist mills seemed to match mine, and he suggested two that I might want to photograph. When I asked whether he knew of any property for sale, he told me that Demon Hately wanted to sell his run-down farm.

Since Uncle Demon honed to go some place before the moon fulled, we soon found ourselves the owners of his old log house with forty acres, more or less, of scrub pine, laurel steeps and fields grown up in broomsedge. The dilapidation was picturesque but sad. Pioneers had raised the solid little cabin, and some woman probably, hungry for beauty, had planted the red rambler rose that flourished against the stone chimney. Now there was only emptiness and a lonesome silence in the clearing.

Years of neglect had left the house a mess. It needed a stout heart and strong back to make the place at all liveable again. But when we rocked on our porch as the sun set and a bird warbled, or we hugged the genial fire forking up the chimney while mists pressed against our door, we felt the serenity enjoyed by the pioneers. Maybe broomsedge does signal worn out soil; I thought it was beautiful.

Our closest neighbors were a kindly, middle-aged couple living just near enough for comfort, and a family with many children on the other side of the woods. Our first visitor, whom I got up one morning to find sitting on the edge of the porch, and who afterward appeared regularly, was a dark skinned, brown-eyed little boy with a painful limp and a permanent scowl. Though not a sunny character, his spirits lifted the merest trifle whenever we raised the echoes target practicing on a tin can hung over a fence post.

Our cabin stood in a little northy cove about a short mile along the swag of ridge west of the Trail home. And whenever we drove the gouted road, I liked to catch a glimpse of Aunt Titia out hoeing her garden patch or sitting on her porch. We always waved. And we were hardly settled when I went over one morning to buy some eggs, on purpose to meet her.

Cynthia Creasman's cabin

Chapter IV

She was nowhere in sight as I followed the path through her tall boxwoods. But the doors stood open wide so that passersby might look straight through the house and out into the sunny green yard behind. And her big stone chimney was smoking.

So light were my footfalls on the trodden earth that I rounded the last box bush and caught a fancy red rooster peeking into the house from the doorsill. He stood there arrested in mid-stride, with one yellow foot upraised and his head cocked, so rapt that he was deaf to my approach until I called, "Hello? Miss Trail?" Then he gave a startled squawk and made tracks.

Aunt Titia stepped to the threshold and stood framed in the doorway. She wore a white cotton headrag knotted under her wrinkled chin, gray calico waist with pins stuck in the bosom, rusty dark woolen skirt sagging behind and fronted with a full apron of faded blue check, and grubby high shoes half laced up.

She was a small woman, and wizened, quietly waiting there with one hand on the door jamb and her blue eyes fixed on me. At first there seemed a chill in our meeting. But to my cheerful inquiry how she did, she managed a wan little smile.

"Jest tol'able well, thank you," she replied. "Come in and set a spell. I'll fetch some cheers."

I climbed the stepstones and helped her inch through the door a heavy rocker. Then there was a stumpy little split-bottomed "settin' cheer" to be lifted out.

She righted the patchwork seat cushins, saying, "The reason why I keep my cheer pads turned over is 'cause the cats gits up in 'em. The purtiest kind of tabby cat come here a while back. And she found two leetle 'uns."

Offering me the rocker, she took the straight chair with its gap from a missing cross-slat that accommodated the hump on her back. Her full skirts spread away, and along one thigh her sweatrag bulged the apron pocket. She sat at ease, her gnarled, dark-veined hands folded in her lap.

I mentioned our purchase of old Demon Hately's sway-backed cabin and little pole barn propped against the wind. And I had been eager to meet her, because I felt like I knew her through Tillie.

"Oh, good gracious," she exclaimed with her crinkly smile. "Well, now, I'm proud you drapped by. I may be old and pore and ugly, but I do love to see people."

"Tillie and I are great friends," I said. "She's the sort of person you just love from the first moment of meeting."

"Yes'm. She's one of God's good women. Ask anybody an' they'll tell you she's got a heart big as a hoss collar."

I reminded her that several times I had passed by and waved.

"Air ye the one? Well, now, I call that pyorely frien'ly."

Afterward she told me how that first meeting of ours peartened her up. It had been "jest one of them mornin's," and with all her botherments she was feeling limp as a wrung dishrag. Then I happened along and made her forget that tart little pain, which like as not was mostly heartache anyway.

"I'm proud you drapped by," she repeated. "Tillie sets sich store by you. And I'll try to enjoy you somehow."

Her old-fashioned speech expressed the hope that she could entertain me.

"There hain't nothin' much a-goin' on hereabouts. Only jest farmin' and housekeepin'. I never done nothin' wuth talkin' about. I never stole nothin'. Ner killed nobody. Though they's times my patience gits sore." She chuckled. "I never had but one had fight. That'as in my school days, and I got the best of hit."

"Just sitting here on such a beautiful morning is pure pleasure for me," I said. The air was vocal with the song of birds, their melodious joy punctuated by the harmony of a wandering cowbell. Down the path two sparrows chirped and fluttered in a little dust bath. As I told her, after a hard winter of too many people, I craved solitude.

"I like fur back," she said complacently. "I like God's nature as He made hit. My pappy had a big scope of land, and I've helt onto most of hit, to kindly wrop me in peace."

And peaceful we were. Not a soul had passed on the road. And sitting there, facing out across the march of finger ridges, one succumbed to a dreaminess in the languid drift of clouds above the blue vague of mountains.

I said, "I admire your distant view."

Oh, hit's fur," she conceded, "but a mite shet in. Ginerally I go a-viewin' up on old Baldy. I take me a seat on a big flat rock and view the whole round world."

"It can't be any more beautiful up there than from here," I insisted.

"Well, they's a heap more of hit. I make out to go a-viewin' about twice't a year. In the Spring I cain't forego them leetle wild strawberries up there that's jest packed full of sweetness. And come the Fall, the tree colors ever'whur makes the purtiest kind of patchwork."

In all seasons the mountains were beautiful, and so were the cabins like hers that fitted the scene so perfectly. I confessed my intention of photographing some of the old buildings that were too rapidly disappearing.

"I jest love me old house," she said gently. "My payrents raised hit on cl'ared land, and hit ain't changed much. Hit'as built 'thout airy nail, but some's bin driv in since. The roof's bin patched, and the winders set in, but aside from them things, hit stands today jest as hit did when hit'as fust built."

Her parents had a sure eye for harmony so that with age the little hut fitted its ledge of earth like it had grown there.

"And I reckon there hain't a better house-seat in these parts," Aunt Titia added. "I want you to try my good freestone water. Hit tastes *the best*."

"Tillie says you've lived here all your life."

"Yes'm. I was borned in this old house. I was the oldest child. My pappy and mammy only had six childern. Four are dead, two livin'. I'm in my eighty-fifth year." She smoothed her white hair back under her headrag and tightened the knot at her chin. "I was the oldest," she repeated. "And as my old pappy uster say, I had to be boy and girl too. Fer of a day I'd be out a-hoein' corn, and of a night I'd spin and weave and knit."

With the blunt toe of her grubby shoe she scratched the back of a young brown tabby that came up on the porch and stretched at her feet. The cat got busy washing her forelegs, pausing between licks to study our faces, her pink tongue lolling.

"Till I got so nocount," Aunt Titia went on, "I never et my breakfast by daylight in my life. Allus by the time light broke, I'd done et and was ready to go milk the cow. When I was through with that, I went to the fields with my hoe or plow or whatever I was a-goin' to use." She heaved a deep sigh. "Lord, I've plowed a-many a furrer. . . I've mowed a-many a swath of hay. . . I've split rails, and all sichlike as that. . ." Absently she twisted a gold signet ring on her second finger. "I've got the will yet, but I hain't got the strength."

"From what I hear, you're equal to most anything," I told her.

"Oh, I do me own work. And long's I've bin in this old house I've toted ever' bit of my water. But I hain't got the stren'th no more to han'le the big bucket. Yonder hit sets bottom up'ards. I have to use the leetle bucket." She pulled out her sweatrag and gave her nose two quick swipes. "I'm thankful I can still cut most of me own farwood. . . 'thout too many misplaced licks. I hoe about an hour or hour and a half; then I'm like a sheep, I stick my head in the shade till sundown."

"Would you like to be sixteen again?"

'No, ma'am! I've seed too much hard work," She gazed a moment into space, then she smiled. "But I'll be truthful with ye. I'd like to be so's I could run and kick up my heels. And dance! Git'n a big ring and promenade all! A-many's the time I've went to a dance after I'd worked in the fields all day. I had power then to what I've got now, yes ma'am."

"I suppose the music hasn't changed much."

"No'm. We had 'Turkey Buzzard', 'Old Dan Tucker', 'Gittin' Upstairs' and 'No Hell in Georgie'. And there was one somethin' about 'she danced all night with a hole in her stockin'.'" Her smile was rueful. "Now my knees is stiff. But a-many a time I've danced a tune with my hand, right on."

Around the corner of the cabin strutted the handsome red rooster. He stretched his neck and crowed lustily.

"You hesh yore mouth, you triflin' pup!" Aunt Titia shouted. "Hit's none of yore business." The bird fixed her with a beady-eyed slant and crowed again. "You'll git the sore throat;" she shouted, adding with her crinkly smile, "That there's Jeremiah. He jest talks to me."

Resting the palms of both hands on her knees, she bent forward to rise. The cat scrambled up and waited expectantly. "Come in," she said, "and let me show you my leetle hut."

Appalachian Folks

Cynthia Creasman

Chapter V

Everything had its little story. Aunt Titia pointed across the weather-fretted edge of the porch to the bottom doorstone. "I've et bread ground on that millstone where they grind corn to make meal," she told me. "My old pappy fetched hit here fer a step."

Tiny green ferns, "trem'lin' fierns" she called them, clustered all around the big granite circle. She had transplanted those from her upper woods. And draping one end of the porch was a fragrant blossoming vine, much like honeysuckle, that screened the shelf for her water bucket and tin wash basin. She reached down a long spray of pale orange bloom. The flower stem piercing an oval leaf upheld four narrow petals side by side with a fifth branching off. "I call hit 'Lady's Hand'," she said. "See the thumb and four fengers?" We both savored its fragrance. "I found hit when I was out a-hoein' my corn."

Evermore a dear lover of flowers, she had fetched it down and tied it up to the house. And a while back, she toted in the trumpet vine that "purtied up" the chimney corner. They went well, she thought, with the shrubs in her yard: the thriving boxwoods, a snowball bush higher than her head, and her Sylvanie Pear. "Seem like a body has to have a few purties," she declared. "One kind or 'nother."

She turned indoors, cautioning me to duck the low door top. "I laugh and tell 'em ever'body has to bow to me when they come in my door. My pappy was only a mite taller than I am. I uster be bigger, but I've growed down."

The cabin's one big room was about evenly divided between her sleeping quarters on the right and, opposite, her arrangements for cooking and eating, with a generous free space left in the middle.

The two wide plank doors opening inward partially screened in each corner a high four-poster, fat-bedded, and dressed in colorful patchwork. Between the beds stood a low chest of drawers, homemade of yellow poplar, its top cluttered with stuffed boxes and odd medicine bottles that crowded a battered alarm clock. Above on the wall hung a pair of tinted photographs in oval frames—a black-bearded man and a faded wisp of a woman.

Aunt Titia dusted over the puncheons ahead of me, pointing out things.

"I've been a-livin' here alone now eighteen year—ever sence my old pappy died—and I never slep' in this corner. I allus sleep in that corner. This'n's jest as good bed, but hit don't lay right."

She smoothed a wrinkle from its cover then faced about. "Folks laughs at the way I sleep. I've got me a rope bed, then they's a straw bed, and on top of that, two feather beds."

In its windowless nook her bed loomed high and mighty: a large framework nearly as broad as it was long, with heavy square posts reaching ceilingward, and cording high off the floor. It had been very ingeniously constructed by her remarkable pappy. Of three, maybe four, kinds of wood—at least there was poplar, maple and pine—and put together without a single nail, it could be dismantled to twenty-four wieldy pieces and moved by any weakling. So Aunt Titia proudly told me.

It wore the gayer quilt, a pattern she called "At the Depot," with lots of red in it. Above, a small shelf was piled high with old shoe boxes yellowed and flyspecked, and tied with strips of washed-out cloth. Underneath gleamed a white chamber pot, and handy to step down on lay a faded little old drugget. At the foot, above a small brown trunk, her drab garments hung on pegs against the dark wall.

"Hit'll be two year, three month and ten days since I slep' away from home," Aunt Titia was saying. "I've been places, and folks had jest as good beds as I've got, but they don't lay right nuther. I tell 'em I'm sorta like an old hen—I git about of a day, but of a night I want to git home to roost."

Some city woman stopping by her door had asked if she was not afraid there all by herself. Insulted, Aunt Titia had answered—

"No, ma'am! I hain't afeared of ary thing. I never lock my doors, and on a hot night I leave one of 'em open. When anybody comes, I allus ask 'em who they air and what do they want. Nobody never bothered me." A slight pause, and then, "Oh, one night about a month ago, a feller come here, and he was drunk. He says, 'Aunt Tish, what ud you do if'n I was to start a-cuttin' up?' I says, 'Why, I'd putt a hole in ye. And if'n you don't believe hit, I'll show ye plainer'n words can tell.' He jest laughed and went on off."

Across the room you faced her big stone fireplace with its cluster of black iron kettles and gray graniteware coffee pot, and its narrow mantel-shelf at such a tilt that it held precariously a single object. This was a small china pitcher painted with pink roses. A strip of faded calico through its handle tethered it to a nail in the wall. Aunt Titia pointed a crooked finger. "That pitcher's a hundert year old. Old age yallered hit. I keep hit tied up so's hit'll not be smashed to flinders on the hearthrock."

Flanking the fireplace were two small and crooked windows curtained with flowered cretonne and admitting the daylight, which probed chinks around the walls not wadded with newspaper.

Iron tongs in hand Aunt Titia fed the fire. "I jest love me old farplace," she said. "I do my bakin' and make pear butter and all sichlike as that, right on. I never owned a cookstove. Vittles don't taste right, cooked on a cookstove."

Ticking away on its own little shelf was her old box clock, "bought forty year ago fer three dollars and been runnin' ever since." It stood above her big table covered with yellow oilcloth and holding odd pieces of china, a jelly glass with spoons thrust in handle first, and a coal oil lamp.

Across the way, her food safe with pierced tin door panels leaned against the boxed-in attic stairs. Beside it she kept a good supply of firewood neatly ranked up. In front stood her big spinning wheel.

Calendar "art," mostly outdated, hung here and there; while from the loft beams in the stair corner depended a string of onions and two bunches of dried herbs.

Having picked up a lard pail and taken in hand her walking stick, Aunt Titia was ready to lead the way to her little cold spring cupped under the hillside in the shade of tall rhododendrons. Ahead of me, she covered ground with even stride and springy step in her run-over shoes.

Amongst her old apple trees stood four hollow log gums around which the bees hummed. "Bees is a heap of comp'ny," she said over her shoulder, "when a body lives alone the way I do. And I like good honey—long sweetenin,' we call hit. I don't want none of this make-out honey. I tell you, when hit comes to vittles, I like to eat good as the next feller. I pick the first strawberry that turns, and the first blackberry... Them old trees of mine still fruit, and long's I'm fit and able to move, I'll git my craps in."

Her log springhouse, shady and cool, sheltered crocks of milk and butter. She spied about for an old toad-frog she said lived there, but he was off somewhere on a "jant". From the clear depths of the spring she lifted a brimful gourd dipper and filled the clean glass she had brought along just for me. It was delicious. "I tell you," she said, "a bold spring of sweet water is the Lord's blessin' on this airth."

I took up the full pail and we started back to the house. Down in the chicken coop a hen was singing. Another began to cackle. And while I waited there in the path, Aunt Titia went to raid the nests. She returned with two brown eggs in the palm of her hand. "Hain't they purty? This'n's Samanthy's, and this'n's Phoebe's."

As we were about to reenter the house, she paused before the door of the leanto, which she called her plunder room. "I'll show ye the corn I made with me own old hoe," she said. We looked in upon a clutter of tools and jars and jugs, with heaps of white and yellow corn, and gourds hanging from the rafters. Scattered about were odd pieces of harness, the leather dried and cracked, and old split baskets, mostly melon shaped. There was a churn that her mother had used, and a broadaxe where it was last laid up by her pappy. Ready at hand were crude scales fashioned from two squares of wood hung by their four corners from the ends of a long wooden pole balanced on center.

With her quavery laugh, Aunt Titia said, "I've got ever'thing in here but a leetle bit of gold."

I said, "You don't seem to miss it."

"Well, I'll tell ye," replied this wise granny. "I hain't a pusson to fritter life a-pinin' fer what I'll not likely git. I jest make do. If'n I git me a leetle somethin', I take hit and I'm thankful. If'n I don't git nothin', I'm thankful I'm able to make do."

Her old clock chimed in, striking noon with wheezing frenzy, and reminding me that I had overstayed.

Aunt Titia said, "Set and I'll fix us a leetle snack."

Another time, I promised. But I had hoped to buy some eggs.

Right then she could spare only four. And she laughed when I put them in my hat.

I told her how much I had enjoyed our visit. And she responded, "You come back and see me soon. Yo're good comp'ny."

Over her doorway, on wooden pegs, rested a rifle that was no rusty old relic. But below, through a hole in the door, her latchstring of twisted brown paper hung outside.

Appalachian Folks

Old Mill Wheel

Chapter VI Titia Trail

Tim Trail and his dauntless first-born enlivened the family chronicle, sharing a special luster in Tillie's recollections. But a true heroine of those cruel times for women was the child-bride Clarinda whose sweetmoon was a nine-day trek through nearly unbroken wilderness. Scarcely fifteen then, and weakly all her life, she ventured far beyond the aid and comfort of her kin, and with a lad just come of age. Never really well, but not too ill to work like a horse, Rindy bore six children and had no time to rest till the day she died.

Aunt Titia summed up her mother's obit one day when she set a spell from her garden work.

"I like to hoe corn," she remarked. "I'd ruther be out in the field as to be in the house. I reckon hard work never hurt nobody. I've seed a-plenty of hit." She fished her sweatrag from her apron pocket and mopped her brow. "When I'as a-growin' up, Pappy put the whole bunch of us out in the cornfield. They'as six head of us. and ever'thing that'as big enough helped. We'd git out right soon of a mornin' and hoe till dinner time. Then Mammy and me ud come to the house and fix dinner. Then while the other'ns was a-restin', we done the housework: made up the beds and washed the dishes. When the other'ns was ready to go back to hoein', we'd go with 'em and hoe till supper time. We never got no time to rest. Most like of an evenin' we'd burn big pine knots and spin or weave."

Rindy's travail left its blight upon her. In her photograph no trace of youth graced her sad countenance, although she was still a young woman. At forty-eight she "went to her reward." And all her burdens fell upon the shoulders of her daughter.

Rindy had been gone now fifty-three years, two months and nine days, but for Aunt Titia she remained a living presence—"I can see Mammy jest as plain as I can see you a-settin' there. I tell you, our folks don't never leave out... less'n we fergit 'em."

My friend sooner forgot the living than the dead. For times when she rested, just nursing her hands, she might take down one of the old shoe boxes from the little shelf above her bed.

"When I'm a-settin' here, and I git kindly lonesome," she told me, "I jest fetch me old box of pitchers out and then hit all goes away."

One by one she turned them over in her gnarled fingers: old tintypes of her father, sharp-eyed and black-bearded, a solid chunk of a man in roomy, wrinkled coat; and the only likeness she had of her mother, plain and gaunt, her deep-set eyes heavy-lidded, her thin lips drooping.

Aunt Titia held her parents side by side. "If'n they ever spoke a short word I never heerd hit.'

She and her mother had been very close—"I never stayed away from my mammy but two weeks in my life till she died, and that was to help out with sickness."

And she doted on her father. His expressions of native wisdom became her maxims. It made her proud that of all his children *she* had been his "pleasure piece." "Pappy allus said he wouldn't trade me fer three fellers."

Toward her mother's frailties Aunt Titia was compassionate. "Mammy was tol'able tall, but the most she ever weighed was one hundert pounds. She warn't much good in the fields. She couldn't never plow. But she'd hoe corn!"

To have endured even her short span, Rindy had to be a woman strong in quiet ways. But from her photograph you would have judged her a spiritless creature. Sitting for her portrait brought her no visible joy; she presented a drab figure, her glance vague, her shoulders sagging. She wore a plain dark dress without frill or ornament, without so much as a small broach at her throat.

But sixteen year old Titia sat for her picture bedecked in all her finery, with rings on her fingers, large earbobs, and at the neck of her light-colored dress a string of beads *and* a broach. She wore her hair drawn back from a center part. The photographer had pinkified her cheeks. Her steadfast gaze and the slight tilt of her head lent her an air of supreme confidence.

"I was thought a right likely gal them days," Aunt Titia reflected. "But you'd not think hit, seein' me now."

"*I* think you're right likely still," I told her. "You're a charmer."

A faint smile betrayed her pleasure. But she was depreciatory. "Oh, I'm jest an old crock. I reckon, though, I orta be thankful I'm alive."

I wondered why, when life for her had been so hard.

"And thankful I've been stout all my time, after me gittin' sich a bad start. When I come into the world a-way early and not more'n half ready, they figgered I'd never 'mount to nothin'." She chuckled. "Pappy said I looked miserabler than a leetle picked bird. Said he plumb deespaired I'd hold out till mornin' even, him bein' all by his lone. But he done the best he knowed how fer me. And," she finished with her quavery laugh, "here I am! Now I've helt out this long, I might mebbe tetch a hundert. The good Lord willin'."

Still, sometimes she felt like she was on her last legs already. "Settin' down," she said, "I feel about fifty. But when I go to git up, I feel a hundert'n fifty." With a shrug she laid aside the image of her vanished youth. "I reckon there hain't no manner of use to be dark-hearted. I cain't change nothin' nohow. So I'll jest make do. I can set by the far, a-thinkin' back'ards and for'ards. I've had joy, and I'm satisfied they's more on the way."

Some of the pictures dredged up from the shoe box she gave scarcely any notice. Emma, her only surviving sister, rated little more than a glance and the briefest mention. Other kinfolks seemed to be of no special interest at the moment.

She did not name for me the handsome young man with roguish eyes, seated by a table and holding a small book. When I asked who he was, she answered indifferently, as if remembrance of him had escaped from her mind, "A cousin of mine," and dropped him back into the box.

Over others she lingered with fond recollections.

The chubby youngster with big wistful eyes and sausage curls was her favorite sister Tempe, who died young. Aunt Titia would have liked the picture of Tempe when she was older, but that one somehow got lost when her young man was found on a high trail dying of the milk sick. They were out looking for him and heard his dog howling.

The face of Uncle Dan'l, a wizened old gent with deeply furrowed brow, thin wispy hair and stingy beard, reminded her of an exciting event when she was hardly older than Tempe in the picture.

"Pappy sometimes tuk me to town with him when he went," she recounted. "Ginerally he left me at Rankin and Pulliam's store. Uncle Dan'l called me his leetle Trix. One day he says, 'Leetle Trix, come 'ere and see the hogs.' They'as a big drove of hogs a-goin' through. The drivers ud crack their whips and holler: 'Whoa! Whoa! Rakum and Pullum!'" She laughed. "I couldn't watch 'em hard enough."

Next she opened a pink paper folder, and smiled. "This here's my old granmaw." She handed me the image of a strong character with snapping dark eyes and lips firmly set—a person of great dignity, with a small waist and billowing skirts. "Granmaw was a leetle bitty old woman, but her back and jest as straight. She allus wore a cap with ruffles and a cape and linsey dress."

She took back the photo and studied it, half smiling. "Granmaw ud weave coverlids. And I had to help her thread the eyes in the harness till I'd git so tard. But they'as no stoppin' her. You jest had to go on. She warn't satisfied to make plain cloth, jest two treadles, ner even jeans that tuk three treadles; she had to make coverlids with *four* treadles. And she'd throw the shettle, tromp the treadle, throw the shettle, tromp the treadle, till you'd might nigh go crazy."

Came the day when little Tish wanted to weave on Granmaw's old loom—"I says, 'Granmaw, let me weave.' She says, 'Law, child, you'll break ever' thread in hit.' I says, 'Let me try.' The fust time I throwed the shettle hit went clar through and fell on the floor. Granmaw picked hit up and handed hit to me. And afore you knowed hit, I'as a-weavin' right on."

With sudden resolution she lifted her picture hoard onto the "settin' cheer" beside her, saying, "Come let me show ye the sweetest coverlid I ever wove."

From the old brown trunk at the foot of her bed, and careful wrapping in one of her own handmade sheets, we drew forth a beautiful creation patterned in gray and rose red. From off her spare bed Aunt Titia lifted a carton of freshly carded wool and tucked it underneath among other boxes where she stored quilts in progress, muttering, "I tell you, when you've got a bed nobody's a-sleepin' in, hit'as a puffec' pack hoss."

We opened up the coverlet for display. It was every bit her own work from start to finish. She sheared the sheep and carded the wool. She spun the thread. Then many an evening after a day's work she wove her pattern by the light of a pine knot. "Madder dyed the red," she explained. "I raised hit and beat the roots up. And I gethered the bark fer the purty dove color."

"It's lovely," I said.

"Hit's a draft called 'True Lover's Knot'." She caressed it with her worn hand and tender gaze. "This here coverlid is sixty-eight year old. And hit's jest as fine as the day hit'as wove. Hit ain't never been used." She backed off to get the effect. "But mebbe the time's come to spread hit on the bed jest fer looks."

"It's too beautiful to keep hidden away," I suggested.

"And ever' breath I draw, my span gits shorter..."

"Surely nobody could love it as much as you do."

"Oh, they's some of 'em been a-devilin' me fer hit." She wagged her head, her jaw set. "I jest told 'em I warn't borned giveaway day."

But her time was running out, and she had her druthers about who got her things. Melissie, she thought, was the one to have her keepsake. "She's my gran' child, and she's not like ary one of t'other'ns. She's a dear lover of purty colors. When she was jest a leetle youngun, hit made her so proud when we putt the kivers out to sun and air, fer they was gaily made. And she bragged how she holp me, when her daddy come to fetch her home."

A decision so painful could wait another day. Aunt Titia began folding up the coverlet. "This here coverlid was finished jest three weeks and two days afore my boy come into the world."

We gathered the treasure into its protective covering.

"I tell you the truth," she said. "Plain talk's easiest understood. I've got a son. I never was married."

Chapter VII

What some innocent had said that riled Aunt Titia I failed to hear; nor did I catch a glimpse of the one who had crossed her. But I was just in time for her sharp retort:

"Yeh, yo're an angel...with horns on yore head!"

And I hesitated there in the path, almost persuaded to turn back. Intrusion might be embarrassing at such a tense moment.

Everyone agreed that Tish Trail was not a person to be trifled with. "She don't take nothin' off'n nobody," they said. "She won't stand fer no funny business."

Uncle Demon, a great one for broguing the countryside and buttonholing you with, "Let me tell you this leetle tale..., gave a gleeful account of the time some outlander was lost and he stopped way up in the night at Aunt Titia's door to ask directions. "That city feller says to me, he says 'That old lady was skeered, I bet.' I says, 'Don't you think hit, Mister. She'd as lief putt a bullet through you as she would a rabbit.'"

Then, to clinch her fearlessness, the old man avowed, "Tish Trail ud frail into Tante Bogus hisse'f, 'gin he come friskin' around."

"Who's Tante Bogus?" I said.

He grinned, "Why, the Old Boy."

Not feeling the devil's brasenness that morning, I was about to leave when Aunt Titia came to her door and caught sight of me. Reluctantly I climbed the stepstones. She looked wretched. But I was welcome. And when we had each "picked a cheer", she launched into her tale of woe—

"Las' night was so quiet, I didn't hear a theng. But somebody stole my chickens."

I was shocked. "Now who'd do a contemptible trick like that?"

"Pink Meaders come past, and he says, 'A fox got our'n.' I says, 'This was a two-legged fox got mine.' I didn't have but four. I ginerally let 'em stay of a mornin' till I et my breakfast. They'd keckle."

I hated to ask—"Jeremiah too?"

She nodded dolefully. "I'll miss the triflin' pup."

Besides the thievery, she had worse worries. Her left hand was bandaged with a strip of faded apron check. "And this mornin'," she went on, "when I squatted down on the hearth, I pitched my hand right into the far. My nails was all crisped up. I got the far out and went to doctorin' right straight." She studied the injured member back and front. "Of a night," she explained, "I save me a chunk of far and bresh the ashes over hit. Of a mornin', I jest bresh the ashes away and there's the seed of my far. But some days I cain't squat down like I uster. I take a swimmin' in my head."

In the fireplace her dinner was cooking in a black iron pot licked by greedy little tongues of flame. Aunt Titia kept an eye on it, lest the forestick burn through.

"Wouldn't a stove make things easier for you?" I asked.

"No, ma'am! Vittles don't taste right, cooked on a cookstove." She got to her feet. "This here's the day you was a-goin' to eat dinner with me."

"It is?" I had to laugh with her.

"Yes'm. I've got us a pot of salat on. I've got a whole mixed multitude. Hit's what they call mustard, a leetle bit of poke, and some lambquarters. You gether hit and parebile hit, then fry hit in grease so's hit'll not be strong."

"I don't want to put you to any trouble," I said.

"Oh, trouble's all they is to anything," she tossed off, her attention on the dinner. "We jest make pleasure out'n hit."

She got busy frying tiny pieces of fatback. Lifting the bits of meat onto a plate, she smacked her lips. "I shore do love fatback fried till hit's right brickle." When the greens were turned into the sizzling skillet, she washed her hands and commenced mixing dough. Rolling it out, she put it in an iron kettle. Between the three feet of the kettle she raked live coals. "So now," she murmured, "we jest kiver him up." On went the lid, already heated, with coals on top.

In no time her bread was done. She served up the salat, and we drew chairs to the table. Except our plates, the food was kept covered.

"My flies is bad mannered," she said, waving them away with her "fly bresh", a green lilac twig.

Her bread tasted very good. It was light and flaky, with crust evenly browned.

But then—

"Mammy allus bragged about my sleight at bread makin'. I holp her the fust time when I had to climb on a cheer to the table." She swished the lilac. "In Civil War times we called cornbread Johnny-constance, fer we had hit weekdays, and biscuit was Billy-come-seldom, 'cause we had them on Sunday."

"Now you can have biscuit whenever you want."

"Yeh, law. Livin's a heap sight easier now than hit was when I'as a-growin' up. Folks don't know what hard times is. Nowadays, afore I git down 'thout a dust of flour on the shelf, my son fetches me a leetle poke. And I make biscuit any day I'm a-mind to. But hit's the contrariness of life, or people, one, that when a feller can have all he wants of a thing, seem like he hain't so greedy fer hit."

One last sip emptied her coffee cup which she carefully set down in its saucer.

"I like your nice old china," I said. "Let me get the coffee pot."

She lifted the cup to catch light on its faded forget-me-nots. "Hit come off'n the Christmas tree over at the Walker place. I got hit fer goin' to Sunday School. And I've drank out'n me own cup all these years." When I resumed my seat, she added, "That's why I like you to come. You don't act like yo're better'n me."

"Better? I think you're wonderful!"

"Well," she confessed, "some folks putts on airs and sniffs their nose up. (I wondered if the outlander of Pink Meaders's store had made her poisonous presence felt.) I don't sniff my nose onless I've got a cold."

"If you catch anybody sniffing," I said indignantly, "just let me know. I'll tell 'em a thing or two."

A little answering smile, and she reached for the jar of her pear butter, freshly opened for me to try. "This here's somethin' new. I've only been a-makin' pear butter fer about twenty-five year. In Civil War times we didn't know nothin' about cannin'. Them days folks dried their fruit." Her thoughts ranged back—

"We didn't suffer too much fer rations in war times. We had our milk and butter, and vegetables and fruit. We raised cane and made syrup. We dried peaches and apples. We picked huckleberries and blackberries, and dried 'em. And we'd not wait till they'as plumb mush ripe, nuther. Them days you didn't pass no house where fruit was ripe but what you'd see a big scaffold and a kiln of rocks with a far under hit, a—dryin' peaches. The children kep' the far a-goin'.

"But I'd ruther to can, or make jelly." She took a last sip of coffee. "And that makes me think, I've got to climb up to the attic and shift my jellies." Carefully she replaced the brown paper cap on the glass of pear butter, knotting the string that kept it in place. "I'm a-gittin' so fergitful I cain't hardly remember the days of the week. I know I git up of mornin', or I wouldn't be a-knockin' about, back'ards and for'ards. And I can remember to go to eat three times a day. But most anything else comes to my mind, d'reckly hit's gone, like a bird a-flyin'."

She wiped her lips on the back of her hand and reached for her little clay pipe.

"I never used terbaccer till I'as almost fourteen year old," she said, jolting her chair around to light the thimble-sized bowl from the fireplace. "Then the doctor give hit to me. Fer a while there, I'd eat my dinner of bread and milk, and go right to the door and spit hit out.

"One day Doc Warren come past and he says to Mammy, he says, 'I've come to eat dinner with ye!'

"She says, 'why, if'n you can putt up with pore folks's rations, yo're welcome.'

"I was a-waitin' on table that day. And when I et my bread and milk, I jest went to the door and spit hit out.

"Doc says, 'What ails you? No wonder yo're like a bone.'

"Then he told me to git a leaf of terbaccer—them days ever'body raised their own terbaccer—and dry hit on the hearth. Then putt hit in a rag and beat hit up and make me some snuff. 'Don't use too much now,' he says, 'so's you git you cain't stop hit.'

"So I done like he said. And fer a while I had to have my leetle pinch of snuff, or I'd begin to belch and spit out my dinner.

"One day I tuk in head to smoke me a pipe. I'as afeared to tetch Granmaw's leetle clay pipe. So I made me a cob pipe. The fust time Granmaw ketched me a-smokin' hit, she give me sich a look—I can see her yet. She never said nothin'. She jest riz up from her cheer and went over to that leetle trunk yonder where she kep' her things. She tuk out her box of pipes and told me to choose one.

"Pappy laughed at me, fer them days the young gals warn't pipe-smokers, as a usual thing. But when we'd et, Granmaw and me ud set by the far and smoke our leetle pipes.

"Hit's pleasured me a heap fer better'n seventy year." She lightly tapped out the ash, then laid it gently on the table. "Nowadays, them leetle bowls is hard to git. But my son knows a feller that keeps me stocked."

After we finished the dishes, Aunt Titia made ready to go to the attic. But we heard a car door slam, and she went to look out. A man's voice answered her chaff about "speak of an angel". As the caller bent through the door, she said, "This here's my son John."

"Howdy, ma'am," he greeted me cordially. A tall man, but thin and wiry, he had lively brown eyes and good teeth. On his way to town, he'd stopped by in case she wanted anything. As he stood on the hearth rolling a cigarette, his cheerful gaze shifted between his mother and me, embracing us both in his warm regard. Out of his overalls bib pocket he took the makings, poured from the flat tin a little tobacco along the paper, rolled it, wet the edges with the tip of his tongue and leaned down for a splinter of light from the fireplace.

Aunt Titia, meanwhile, rummaged through papers in a white china pitcher, muttering, "I'm gittin' so fergitful, I have to putt hit all down in writin'."

She settled her specs on her nose. One lens was shattered.

I said, "How'd you break your glasses?"

"Why, I stepped on 'em."

"But you can't read with them that way."

"Oh, I jest peep through the cracks," she joked.

"You'll put your eyes out," I scolded. "Here, I'll write you a note. You go in with John to my father's office and have your glasses fixed."

"But..."

"No buts about it." I was already scribbling: "Miss Trail needs new glasses. Please fix up my friend." I handed her the slip of paper. "This will be your birthday present."

Chapter VIII

In the comfort of her fond recollections Aunt Titia lived happily with those dear departed family members who peopled her lonely moments. But she manifested no sisterly affection for the only other surviving child of her parents. She and Em had not lived under the same roof since the latter was married at fifteen. They rarely saw each other. And on the subject of Emma, my friend was strangely reticent. No shared pleasures of their girlhood lingered in her mind for telling, as was the case with Tempe.

Two little boys had no life to speak of, both having died in their infancy. Aunt Em was the fifth child. After her came a brother who was "a leetle bit deformed and a leetle bit silly—best lookin' face of all the Trails, mebbe, but his mind never was right". He remained a child, and Aunt Titia took care of him, till he was forty years old, when he was killed by a tree falling on him. For the poor unfortunate, Aunt Titia had sympathy in generous measure, but she felt none at all, apparently, for Emma.

I first met Aunt Em when I went looking for some old buildings and stopped to inquire directions of her man, Watt Ballard. He knew all that country round about, I'd been told, and could probably call to mind any remaining cabins hidden away in remote coves.

Watt Ballard was a big land owner and kept cattle. He got most of the land from his wife. She had the money. Her first husband was a tightwad, according to Uncle Demon: "He never let go o' nothin' till he turned up his toes to the daisy roots."

From just inside her kitchen door Aunt Em watched me drive into the yard. Her home was a large weathered frame house in the valley close to the main road. She stepped onto the porch and responded to my greeting.

"No'm," she said, "Mr. Ballard ain't here. He's gone to town."

"Do you expect him back soon?"

"No'm. He's ginerally allus gone." Her voice was whiny. "Of a mornin' when he's et his breakfast, I say, 'I bet yo're a-goin' to town.' And he allus does."

She was a sorry creature. There remained no trace of the rather pretty Emma in Aunt Titia's picture hoard. She had yellowed gray hair in a tight knot, pale red-rimmed eyes, and the creases about her mouth were darkened with snuff juice. Her saggy dress of lavender print had a pink facing around the hem, part of which was ripped loose and hanging down. Except that her clothes were clean, she looked as woeful as the cats on her porch: a scrawny tom stretched out asleep, and further off, a mangy mother nursing two half-grown kittens with sore eyes.

I asked whether *she* knew of any old landmarks that I might photograph.

She shook her head. No, she couldn't think of any old cabin or mill, right off.

"Well, thanks," I said. "I'm sorry Mr. Ballard isn't here. I thought he might know of some."

"He mought," she said indifferently. "But he ain't here. He's ginerally most allus gone some'eres."

"And you don't know of any?" I asked again.

She gazed vaguely towards the horizon and combed her lank hair with her earthy fingernails. "Wal, no, I don't right off."

"Thanks." I turned to go.

Suddenly she perked up. "I've got a cabin over yonder in the holler. Nobody's a-livin' in hit." She stepped down into the yard. "Hit's right between them leetle hills."

"Can I see it from the road."

"Yes, you can see hit from the road."

"Thanks very much."

She trailed after me across the yard. "Won't you come in and stay awhile?"

"Not this time, thanks."

"Wal, you'll find my leetle cabin over yonder in the field. Hit'as built way back in olden times."

"Thanks." I opened the car door.

"I'll tell my man you was here," she droned. "You best ud set and rest yoreself while. He *mought* come."

"I'm afraid I can't wait for him."

"Stay, and I'll fix us a leetle snack." She smiled wistfully.

"Thank you, but I really must be getting on."

Her face forlorn, she sagged where she stood, watching me drive away.

Chapter IX

The morning being fit, Aunt Titia had been out hoeing her corn in her usual fashion: she'd hoe a spell, then set a spell. "But these days," she lamented, "I cain't hoe so long, and I have to set longer."

Still, she had such a lot to be thankful for. "I've got me a good sound stomick," she boasted. "When hit comes dinner time, I jest eat a dog's bait. I never git the dyspepsy like some old people do. I can eat jest about anything." Smugly she puffed on her little clay pipe.

A wart that "riz up" dark and ugly on her cheekbone was bothersome. Not that it hurt, it was just in the way; she kept fingering it absent-mindedly. "And hit's jest one more blemish on my nat'ral beauty," she said, laughing.

She paused to examine it in the wavy glass of a small mirror hanging beside the fireplace. Her face was withered as a winter potato, and freckled with brown age spots, but her deep-set eyes under pale thin brows were very blue.

She had in mind that we would go to the attic and shift her jellies. But first she wanted to show me her garden which was doing well.

Moving toward her upper door where the noonday sun beat down, she plucked from one knob on the high back of her rocking chair a floppy straw hat. Clapping it on her head, she said gaily, "If'n there's one thing I won't do, hit's spile my complexion."

Along the shade-dappled path she stepped briskly, prodding the earth with her stout walking stick. Honeysuckle and climbing roses lifted their fragrance. There came to us the hum of her bees and the deep tones of the cowbell.

"I tell you," she said, "the Lord orta made me a mole, I love to dig in the ground so. I jest love my gyarden. I'd ruther to be out-a-hoein' hit as anything I know. I like to visit my plants right soon of a mornin' and see how much they growed in the night."

Hers was a tidy patch, with fat onion stalks, cabbage and tomato plants, bean vines and potatoes in flower, all flourishing in rows straight and clean, as were the plantings in her field of green corn already a foot high.

Besides the joy of her plants, her garden afforded a view out to far horizons that lifted the spirit. And while she gloried in the peacefulness of her solitary life, among the corn rows you became aware that the old lady was not wholly beyond the reach of humanity. Though no rooftree appeared through the foliage at the foot of her mountain, there was life down below. And sounds carried in the still air. You could hear voices and laughter of children, a hen cackling and a dog barking.

As we leaned against the rail fence, Aunt Titia said, "Come next week and they's a day fit, I aim to climb up Old Baldy fer my strawberries. Most ginerally they's sich a lavish of fruit up there that a body cain't hardly find steppin' room."

"How far is it?" I asked.

"Oh, 'bout four mile."

"Round trip?"

"One way. Eight mile round trip." She flicked an appraising glance over me. "I spec I could walk you down. Walkin' limbers yore j'ints, and I've footed hit a-many a mile in my time. I walked to town when I was seventy-nine year, two month and ten days old. Hit's a leetle less'n fourteen mile, and hit tuk me a few minutes over three hours. I don't remember the minutes, but I started from home afore seven and I was on the Squar' at ten."

"Did you walk back?"

"No'm. I ketched me a ride. A young feller that said he'as a reporter wanted to take my pitcher. He says, 'And you come from Laurel Fork!' He says, 'How do folks live up there?' I says, 'They live by drawin' their breath!' So then he says, 'How you aimin' to git back?' I says, "Oh, somebody'll give me a lift.' So he brung me home."

As we started back to the house, she said with her crinkly smile, "That there trip like to a-broke me up. I spents twenty cents. I got two oranges. And they'as a big piece of candy in a store. I says to myself, 'I never et one of them, but I'll try hit.' Hit cost me ten cents."

Restoring her hat on the rocker knob, she reawakened the fire with a stout log, then climbed ahead of me up her steep and narrow attic stairs.

"In the wintertime," she explained, "I keep my jellies clost to the chimley where hit's a leetle bit warm. Then come summer, I push 'em back over in that corner under me old tree where they's a pool of shade."

Daylight entering through wide cracks across the boarding of the gables revealed an assortment of house-pluder and family treasures stored in the attic. Things were packed away in boxes. On the seat of a broken chair lay a set of worn wool cards and her pappy's wooden lasts for making shoes.

I persuaded Aunt Titia to take an empty chair while I moved the jellies near by. She picked up first one and then another for close inspection.

"Them's fall grapes I putt up." She peered at something dark in green glass. "You wash 'em, pour molasses on 'em, and putt 'em in yore jars. To start with, you putt molasses in the bottom of the jar, then a layer of grapes, then more molasses till hit's full. You let hit set till tomorrer, then you dreen the molasses off, and you bile 'em."

"Sounds like a lot of work," I murmured. Grapes in molasses didn't appeal to me.

"Oh, but they's plumb tasty," she insisted.

Some of the jellies had been kept so long that she couldn't remember what kind they were. They filled a variety of containers, whatever she happened to have on hand. A pressed glass goblet held an amber-colored jelly. Aunt Titia lifted the newspaper cap. Green mold covered the top and it smelled of wood smoke. Each jar she uncovered released the humble incense of her fireplace cookery.

While in the attic, Aunt Titia wanted to turn over her quilts and check for damage from mice or weather. Two short-legged chairs stood side by side, and across their seats were folded her collection covered with an old raggedy relic. The work in that pile spanned nearly three-quarters of a century. On the bottom lay a quilt started when Tempe was a child just learning to sew. Above rose a heap of newer patchwork, the last so recently finished that she hadn't named it yet.

Least colorful was the ancient one, its pallet muted by time. But it preserved history almost as good as a book. The back a snuff color that wouldn't show soil, its top saved many small remnants of dress goods from garments of all the Trail womenfolk. Though just "a common quilt", with old-fashioned prints mingled hit-and-miss, great variety of design had emerged from the scrapbag. There were checks and plaids and stripes, and polka dots large and small. Across a triangle of deep blue spread streaks like lightning. Over a white piece crawled little black ticks. Pinwheels and shooting stars and frost ferns mingled with leaves and flower patterns. There was even a nautical touch in the white anchors on navy ground.

"Now this'n looks dirty," Aunt Titia commented when she opened it up after checking all down through the pile. "But hit ain't. That is, from be'in used. Nobody hain't never laid under these quilts. They'as jest spread on the bed to see how they looked when they'as finished."

The old quilt smelled a trifle musty, but marvelously it had survived heat and damp for so many seasons in that airish attic filled with dirt-daubers' nests, where chirping birds flew in and out, and the mice might find haven.

For Aunt Titia it evoked memories- "I've wore a-many a waist of them plaids, and a-many an apern of them checks." She pointed to a scrap of brown broken by tiny squares of faded gold and sprinkled with snowflakes. "My old granmaw had a cape of that," she said. "And," touching a piece of black with bearded wheat design in white, "a dress of that."

Her roving glance found a square of mellowed blue crossed by narrow bands like delicate lacework. "One day Pappy was a-goin' to town, and he says, "Well, Tishie, you want me to bring ye the goods fer a dress?' I says, 'Oh, Pappy, you know I'm allus keen about a new dress.' And that'as what he brought."

Her newer quilts were not crazy but neatly patterned and happily named. With small stitches they had been quilted "on the seam and by the piece". There was "Trail Around the Mountain," "Dove in the Window," Chips and Whetstones".

"They'as a feller come by here last year and asked me if I sold my quilts." Aunt Titia was laying them across chair backs and over the tops of boxes. I says, 'Sometimes I do.' He said he'd give me a dollar fer about four of 'em. I says, 'Do you think that's the wuth of 'em?' He says, 'I do.' I says, 'I'd go out yonder and git me a pile of bresh and spread all my quilts on hit and set far to 'em afore I'd sell 'em to you. I warn't borned giveaway day!'"

She kept separating them, and talking. Folks ask me why I make so many quilts. Well, I do hit to enjoy myself. I says, 'I may not live long enough to wear 'em out, but we hain't all a-goin' to die the same time. And after I'm gone, them that's still here can use 'em."

When in all their gay coloring and fanciful patterns her handiwork lay spread before us, Aunt Titia gave voice to a notion lurking in her headpiece. "Now," said she, "I want you to pick yoreself out a quilt. Hit'll be a keepsake from me."

This unexpected generosity from one "not borned giveaway day" caught me by surprise. I demurred. "Oh, you shouldn't give away so much painstaking work," I said.

"I want you to have it," she insisted. "If'n I cain't give hit welcome, I won't give hit atall."

"I can have any one?"

"Yes'm. Ary'n."

I studied them. The nasal whine of a mud wasp filled the interval of silence. Hesitantly, since it was the memorable one, I asked for the old quilt.

She was quite willing. "That'n's the one you want?"

"Yes. I'll be seeing Granmaw in her cape, and you in your blue dress."

And the awkward stitches, drawing puckers here and there, would tell of a little girl's first sewing lessons under the guidance of her devoted big sister.

When we had carefully folded and wrapped up her hoard of covers and were starting below, Aunt Titia thrust into my hand the pressed glass goblet of amber-colored jelly.

"Be keerful now," she cautioned as I preceded her down the ladder-like stairs, "fer I've got nothin' but a death trap here."

Chapter X

It was dark as a pocket at Aunt Titia's. But one dim-lit window and a bright crack around the door quickened the looming shadow that was her cabin. I stumbled over the sprangled tree roots and up onto the porch where I knocked and called her name.

Presently there was a stirring inside, and my little old friend opened the door. At first she couldn't make out who I was. Then she said heartily, "Well, come in. Take you a cheer."

There was a scurrying of soft paws. The kittens, a black and a tabby, were frolicking.

"I was afraid I'd find you abed," I said.

She laughed. "Why, bless you, I don't go to bed till I have to. I read anything in the world I git aholt of. Last winter I might nigh ruin my eyes a-readin' way late of a night—*True Romances* and *Dream World* and all sichlike as that."

Her magazine and spectacles lay on the yellow oilcloth under the lamp with its wick turned high, and her hickory chair was drawn close to the table. I had interrupted her reading *True Romances*.

But it was her birthday. And I came by from town because I wanted to wish her many happy returns and give her some quilt material I had brought.

She took her seat and unrolled the cloth across her knee, threatening to "whup" me if she found no red prints. But I had remembered her favorite color. "You mustn't mind me," she said with her crinkly smile. "I have to have my leetle joke. I've got no time fer folks that has to mouch and moo, and set with their mouth all pouched up fenger-length long." She examined each piece of fabric, commenting on the pretty patterns.

The lamplight gleamed in the frowse of her snowy hair like a halo about her head. It lighted her tidy table, the white cloth covering her dishes, and the spoonholder surrounded by several jars of jelly left outside. It brightened her new tin dishpan hanging on its nail against the wall, and the face of her old clock loudly ticking the minutes away. Dimly, in the far corner, it touched her bed with the covers turned down, and the white chamber pot underneath.

Her fireplace was dark and nearly lifeless, with only a spark caught in a smoldering chunk, seed of the next morning's fire.

The kittens romped energetically, getting under Aunt Titia's chair and into her full skirts. She reached down and slapped them away. "Don't be a-scratchin' my legs!" A switch lay on the oilcloth. "They cut sich rustics," she said, "that I keep me a hick'ry clost by to tingle 'em with."

But already the pair had scampered out her upper door, left open to admit the balmy night air and the moths that fluttered about the lamp. Outside, the insects chorused and katydids rasped their insistent telegraphy. A vagrant breeze fingered the foliage.

I was eager to hear about her birthday celebration. That day, the twenty-third of July, she turned eighty-five. Plans had long been brewing for a big gathering.

But the party was not to her liking. "I didn't want to go to the birthday dinner," she confessed, "'cause I figgered they'd be a passel of drunks there. As hit was, one feller was drunk. He fell down and throwed his hand in one of the cakes. They picked him up and carried him down under a tree. He laid there and went to sleep.

She slapped the kittens out of her skirts. They found an old hickory nut and rattled it over the puncheons.

"Hit's the Lord's blessin' I never married," Aunt Titia added severely. "Fer if'n I'd a-married a drunk man, I'd a-kilt him or he'd a-kilt me, one. Fer I cain't stand a drunk man...

"I never seed my pappy a-staggerin' round the house with liquor. Oh, he'd take a leetle dram, but not more'n a tablespoonful. Them days and times, folks made what they called their bitters. They made 'em from yaller root, lion's tongue or wild cherry bark. Ever' morin' afore breakfast they tuk their swaller of bitters. Hit give 'em an appetite, like a tonic."

She laid her hand on the cat hickory, but the kittens had pranced off again.

"Burdock roots makes the best bitters," she resumed. "And if'n you bile hit, hit makes the best tea fer a body that's bothered with risin's. Horse mint is good fer a cold. And wide dock and narr' dock makes good salat. I tell you, ever'thing on airth is good fer somethin', if'n we only knowed hit."

"Then the party wasn't a success?" I said.

"Well, in a manner of speakin'." She gave me an arch look. "I almost got me a sweetheart. He smiled at me, and I thought hit meant somethin'. But they'as another women slid in afore me."

"Why didn't you take him away from her?"

She chuckled. "Well, I tell ye. He's like me; he ain't so purty."

"But a man's a man," I teased.

"Well, they's men, and *men*," she countered. "And I've got my druthers. When Pappy died, they asked me why I didn't marry. I says, 'Well, hit's hard enough to take keer of one, let alone two. And I was afeared I'd git me a man I'd have to take keer of."

The works of her old clock sort of turned over and fell down inside, and its frenzied striking of ten hustled me off. Aunt Titia fetched the lamp to the door to light me down the path. Reluctantly I left her there alone, such a frail-looking little old lady, holding the light above her head, her humpbacked shadow grotesque on the half-open door. The circle of radiance reached from yard grass to oak leaves. A lone cricket chirped by the stepstones.

Chapter XI

After a morning of heavy rain, fog shrouded the mountains, pressing against the cabin doors. Aunt Titia was busy spinning. Her high wheel stood out in the room before the fireplace. She had spun enough thread to fill one broach. Another was just started. Within reach lay the long thin rolls of carded wool.

She was spinning now for a cousin, but with difficulty. "The wool's sorta bad," she said. "Hit's got long hairs in hit that makes hit break."

To me, the room felt chilly, for there was little more than a spark of fire. But Aunt Titia's work kept her warm.

Using her spin-stick—"so's not to wear out my fingers a-turnin' hit"—she started the wheel, then backed off, drawing out the twist of white wool in her left hand. Her motions were graceful. And she made a picture there in the gloom of the cabin, such a withered little old crookback, her dun-color headrag slipping off her white hair, her greenish dark skirt sagging behind, her grubby high shoes run-over at the heels. The creak and rattle of the wheel drowned out conversation, but Aunt Titia silenced it frequently to rest.

"My old wheel's sorta crazy," she said, tightening the knot of her headrag and tucking back stray locks. "Ever' youngun that comes has to play with hit. I told 'em hit made fuss enough that ever'body a-goin' the road ud think I had a threshin' machine."

She fetched another box of carded wool from her spare bed. "I shore do love to git aholt of me old wheel and cyards. The fust furniture I remember in my mammy's house was a wheel. I larnt to spin when I warn't big enough to reach the broach. Mammy tuk out one of the puncheons and set the wheel through the hole down on the ground. And afore you knowed hit, I'as a-spinnin' right on."

Though now her wheel was worn and warped, and in places tied up with string, it still spun good thread.

"When I'as a-growin' up," Aunt Titia added, "I spun my four cuts a-many a night. Most like, we'd throw a big pine knot in the far and spin or weave till ten or 'leven o'clock, sometimes after we'd worked in the fields all day. And a-many's the night I've wove a web of cloth. I had eyes then to what I've got now, yes ma'am."

"What's a cut?" I asked.

"When the reel goes around one hundert times, hit cracks like a clock. That's a cut."

"What a help," I said. "Imagine having to count."

"Oh, a-many's the time when the cracker was broke on me old reel, I've jest hiked my foot up right that-a-way and stuck my broach down in my shoe and counted right on."

Of the hardy breed that makes do, Trails never let work lag. And now, the mere thought of it all, years and years of it, made Aunt Titia bone tired. She sagged into the little "settin' cheer", her broomstick arms resting in her aproned lap, straight out along her thighs.

"Lord," she signed, "I've beat the old flax till I wouldn't a-keered if they warn't another bit. I've cyarded till I could a-cried like a whupped child fer the misery in my shoulders... I tell you, my payrents shore larnt me to work.

"But now," her smile was thin, "with the neuritis in my back, I'm sorta like a cow eatin' a grin'stone—I have to take hit slow and easy."

Uncle Joe Chambers, Whittemore Branch

Chapter XII

Until shortly before we met that springtime of her eighty-fifth year, Aunt Titia could boast that since a spell of fever in her girlhood soon after her son was born she had not had a pain "more'n finger-length long".

But during the previous winter various old age troubles commenced to plague her. And she fretted—"seem like when one thing turns loose of me, somethin' else grabs aholt."

With her kin she had to keep "secrety" about her ailments, else they'd have her sitting moodily in somebody else's chimney corner. Most of them figured at her age she wasn't long for this world, and they kept deviling her to give up living by herself. But she shrugged them off.

"I'd ruther have my satisfaction," she insisted, "and one leetle meal a day in me own old house. I'm jest too antic and sot in my ways to go a-traipsin' off into other folks's home where I'd be allus in somebody's way."

Tillie, spying out the chinks not wadded with newspaper, gently spoke of the dangers. "This old house is so open, Aunt Tish. One of these days when it's right cold and snowy, you'll ketch yore death."

Aunt Titia was unmoved. "Oh, twixt me old farplace and the old feather bed I'll keep snug jest like allus."

Somebody else remarked that a ripsnorter could cave in the building and smash her to poultice.

Aunt Titia met the tilt. "Oh, I know the old house is kinder shacklin'," she snapped. "But if hit lasts as long as I do, then hit can fall down. I won't mind."

Even Emma, I'd heard tell, had her little say. "Hit don't hardly make sense to contrary providence, Tish. Yo're a-livin' on borried time."

"*Any*body my age," Aunt Titia retorted, "is a-livin' on borried time. I aim to borry mine the best way I'm able, and I aim to borry all my credit'll 'low!"

As it turned out, her credit was first rate. For she borrowed a goodly span. And mostly she made out to spend it the way *she* wanted, though times it took the dumb balkiness of a mule, and again, just plain speaking. When feelings were hurt, Aunt Titia remained philosophical. She made no apologies. "Hit don't never do to swaller anything after you belch it up," she declared. "Hit ain't good fer yore stomick."

Doc said once, they needn't to worry. The only way they'd get rid of her would be to take an iron bar and hit her in the head with it.

She told him they'd have a plenty to do while they were doing that.

"Long's I'm fit and able to move," she vowed, "I'll stay right here in me own old house. When you live in one place a long time, then you can heap yore nastiness in one pile."

Though I shared her trials and forebodings that summer, with the others she strove to keep up appearances. She was not a complainer, it being in her mind that folks didn't want to hear about your aches and pains. But her shortcomings sometimes disgusted her to plaintive lamentation:

"I cain't shoulder a peck of corn no more. Seem like if'n I could jest go like I uster, plow and hoe corn, and cradle wheat...But now I hoe my corn a leetle while, then I git the weak trembles; so I come in and set a spell."

It was during her "settin' spells" that I shared her vistas of memory.

"Comes a downy rain," she remarked one dampish afternoon, "and I'm in the house, I'll be a-pilferin' to see what I've got."

She had come across her old Blueback Speller. It was in bad shape. "The book worms et hit," she said. But it set her mind backward to "the time of books".

"I went to school four or five year. But I was out a lot. Come wash day, I'd have to stay home and help Mammy with the washin'. I allus liked readin'. But I fell out with 'rithmetic. And now I've fergot half I ever knowed."

"So?" I shrugged. "We need remember only what we need."

She gazed a moment into the fire. "I remember the times we had. Good times. School lasted four month. Hit shet up two weeks durin' fodder-pullin' so's the young uns could help. If'n you was in ABC's, hit cost fifty cents; higher up, seventy-five cents and a dollar.

"In school we set on puncheon benches—split logs. Hit'as in the big old log house over on the Locust Knob. And you'd better not come up without yore lesson. If'n you did, they'd set you in the dunce corner and anybody could laugh at you that wanted to.

"One day the gal that set right in front of me let out an awful crack. The teacher thought hit'as me. He throwed the hick'ry right down by my feet. 'Now,' he says, 'you fetch me that hick'ry, fer I'm a-goin' to whup you.'

"I says, 'Now that I'll not do, fer,' I says, 'my pappy and mammy never sont me to fetch a hick'ry when they'as a-goin' to whup me, and I'll not do no more fer you than I do fer them.'

"When hit come dinner time, twelve o'clock, I straddled my legs as fur acrost that hick'ry as I could, jest fer manners.

"And one of the boys—Jonny Lindsay was his name—he told the teacher he was about to whup the wrong one, fer I never done hit."

Chapter XIII

One fine day I drove over to Locust Knob. The quiet road snaked upward through rhododendron and hemlock, with maples and gums and poplars gaily colored, till it came to an end at the cabin door of the Allens, a family once numerous but now reduced to three elderly spinsters.

Beside the way, the old hewn log schoolhouse stood in a small sunny clearing, its drowsy peace scarcely fretted by the "trinkle" of the branch, the sough of the wind in tall pines, and the papery rustle of dead leaves still aloft. Abandoned after many long years of school during the week and church on Sunday, the humble structure remained a memorial to the children now gone quite as eloquently as the scattering of gravestones told of their elders resting on the slope opposite. For names and initials were carved reach-high on the log walls.

Reading these, alone there in the solitude that was enlivened only by the grasshoppers spraying out before me as I tramped through the weeds, I tried to conjure up in imagination the scenes of bygone school days when big and little boys cast sheep's eyes at the girls.

"When we'as younguns a-goin' to school," Aunt Titia had told me, "all in one fam'ly tuk lunch in one dinner bucket. Then when dinner time come, one ud say, 'I got apple pie. Who'll eat hit with me?' Sharing treats, I gathered, was "the thing". And special friends all had nicknames.

The old school's weathered log walls kept a permanent roll of many boys. Even Demon Hately's name was there—Demon X Hately—though I knew that he never went to school a day in his life. The old man could neither read nor write. On documents requiring his signature he made his mark.

The hewn face of one mossy log, a good two feet across and second from the ground on the sunny south wall, had been appropriated in part by a lad evidently man enough to discourage encroachment on his message to the world. There he had carved a big heart, deep cut and lasty. And closed together within were two names: Jonny Lindsay—Tish Trail.

At once the old romancer in me commenced to ruminate. Jonny Lindsay figured largely in Aunt Titia's reminiscences.

There was the time he got to acting the fool riding an ox. "Them days," she said, "nearly ever' fam'ly had an ox. Hit done their plowin' and their haulin'. Pappy had two. Now when an old ox begins to wrinkle up his back, you'd better git off, fer he's a-gittin' ready to putt his head down and pitch you off. Well, we had a bad storm and the branch was up, and hit left water a-standin' in the road. Hit made a bad place and a long one. Jonny Lindsay he come along a-ridin' an ox. Like common, he was a-cuttin' up, and not a-payin' his ridin' critter no mind. Right in the middle of that muddy hole the ox wrinkled up his back and threw Jonny on his head. He come up lookin' like a motley-faced calf. And I jest had a laughin' fit."

Her levity seemed not to have quenched the young man's ardor, for there was another memorable time—

"Him and me met in the road one day. He says, 'I hear tell you can play the jew's-harp.' I says, 'Oh, I pick at hit a leetle.' I says, 'You got a repytation yoreself.'

'Oh,' he says, 'I fetch a tune now'n agin.' I says, 'well, if'n you got ary'n about ye, start hit up.' He says, 'I allus tote one in pocket. I'll play you down.' I says, 'I allus tote one too. I'll go ye fer twenty-five minutes.' We played together fer I reckon nigh on to an hour. He says, 'All right, I couldn't git ahead of ye.'"

As I turned away from the telltale heart, Uncle Demon trudged up the road with a scythe on his shoulder. I had chosen that day after he mentioned that he was coming over to mow the weeds in the burying ground. "Tish Trail shamed me to hit," he grumbled.

I joshed him about his name big as life on the schoolhouse wall, and him never a day inside the door for learning.

He turned his little pale eyes on his handiwork. "Wal, I had to leave my mark some'eres, didn't I? A feller named Jonny Lindsay drawed off the letters fer me atter I'd done made the X with the curlicues."

"Was Jonny Lindsay a friend of yours?"

"Wal, in a manner of speakin'," he drawled with a wink. A tic caused his left eye to wink at odd times, even when he was dead serious. "Jonny was a friend to ever'body." Uncle Demon lifted his misshapen hat and scratched his tousled head. He was a small man in ragged overalls, with a homely face and big ears that stuck out. His hair needed cutting, but he kept his chin clean shaven. "I couldn't nowise keep up with his larkin'," he said. "I didn't stand no chancst with the gals, 'longside o' him. Jonny was the kind o' feller had 'em all moony."

"He seems to have fallen for Aunt Titia Trail," I remarked. "His heart is on the schoolhouse wall."

"Yes'm." Uncle Demon leaned on his scythe, ready for talk.

"Was Aunt Titia a pretty girl?"

"Yes, ma'am! She had har the color of corn tossels, and them blue eyes..."

The old man's face beamed. His gaze wandered from me to the puncheon log that crossed the branch. "I ricollect one day I shammicked this-a-way 'long about time school let out. Jonny he come a-bustin' out the door jest a-oozin' deviltry. He sashayed out thar on that footlog. Wal, hit'as kinder slippery and he fell kersplash in the water." The exquisite comedy tickled him still. "Wal, the other'ns run to pull him out, but he didn't git off 'asy. They ketched him in a big ring and they wouldn't let him go till he told 'em who his sweetheart was. Wal, Jonny he throwed a devilish look all around and he says, 'Tish Trail, hit's you!'"

"What did she do?"

"Turned her back on him. Jest fer manners. Hit'as only jest calf love, I reckon. Nothin' never come of hit," he said soberly, and winked.

"Is he still around?"

"Yes'm. He runs the mill on Carver's creek." The old man lifted his scythe. "Tish Trail'll jower me if'n I don't git them thar weeds cut."

Over in the burying ground lay Uncle Demon's wife Dovey. She had a small white stone that bore a poignant message:

> Mother is gone
> but not forgotten—
> she is resting in the arms of
> Jesus waiting for her
> loved ones to come.

Her spouse stood gazing down at the overgrown grave. He wiped his mouth with a crooked forefinger, then hooked his thumb under his overalls suspender. "Fifteen year ago my wife died," he said, again straying from his mission, "and I hain't done nothin' sence. I'd git married if'n anybody ud have me." A wink. "I'm peart yet."

They told of Uncle Demon that he was a morsel beside his wife who in later years weighed twice what any women ought. But she was a worker. They married young and began their wedded life by walking thirty miles to visit kinfolks. Then he got a job earning 40 cents a day and she was paid 25 cents. After a time, with a little nest egg, they settled down to farming, and for nearly forty years Uncle Demon hauled produce to market, driving an ox to a small schooner wagon.

The old man's glance measured the grave from head to foot, and moved him to reminisce. "She was the hardes' woman I ever undertuk to ketch." He propped himself with the scythe. "I got her out o' Yancey. A cousin o' her'n tol' me about her. He says, 'You allers was a lover of women,' he says, 'an' she's the purtiest flower that ever bloomed out.'

"Sometimes of a Sunday evenin' I'd go over and set with her a spell. Then I picks up my hat and goes over to see another'n. I never would set aroun' with jest one. 'Come back and see me when you git ready,' she'd allers say.'" He gave me a simple little smile. "She was the hardes' women I ever undertuk to ketch."

Eventually in his casual courtship, he got around to proposing. "One evenin' I jest says to her, I says, 'I'm a-goin' to git me a wife. How about hit? You wanna make me one?'"

So they got hitched and raised a big family. Of the dozen or so children, most were dead, and the others had scattered to "furrin'" parts. Nobody seemed to know where they were. And the old man was left by himself.

He lived first one place and then another, helping out with the farming. In spare time he wandered over the countryside like a stray dog. Folks seemed to be generous if he happened by at meal time. One noon when I met him after he'd stopped at a house, I noticed a strange bulge under his arm. I said, "What you got in your shirt?"

"Bread," he answered with a grin. "Want some?"

Yet the old fellow was not destitute. The sale of his patrimony had enriched him. Land acquired by his father about the time little Demon was born, "for and in consideration of the sum of *five cents* for every acre," had cost my father ten dollars per. Most of the money Uncle Demon had deposited in his personal banking system, a bean can buried among the grasping roots of some sentinel tree. His wants just then didn't call for a spending spree, and the cash would come in handy when he found the wife he kept looking for.

"I'd want me a young gal," he said, very serious, "and not one that ud go off and leave me a-cryin'. I'd set and fan her all the time, and feed her squirrel and candy..." His expression was beatific. "Mary Pickford, she lives in Californy. I got her pitcher she sont me. She's a purty gal. But," plaintively, "I don't know her."

He lifted his scythe. "I'd send her my pitcher, but I don't take a good pitcher. My eyes is too small and crowded close together."

Uncle Joe Chambers' neighbors cradling his wheat

Chapter XIV

Though I lacked her experience in fireplace cookery and could offer only stovetop vittles, I invited Aunt Titia to dinner before we closed up for winter in town. And she accepted. John brought her over, dressed in black sateen, with a flat, wide-brimmed hat of black braid, and her shoes shined.

I showed her our little hut. And we laughed again over the mishap getting in a small truck-load of secondhand furniture. We hadn't brought much—only two beds, two tables and four chairs, including a couple of rockers. Evenso, everything fell through nearly down to "Chiny", as our driver remarked. The rattly old fliver chugged and snorted over outcroppings of rock and crisscross gullies, some of them washouts, others clogged with loose stones that gave way under the wheels. The load swayed precariously, threatening to topple into the ditch, but each time miraculously righted itself. We managed to labor on till one final deep gash caught us right to the axle, and there everything hung at a crazy tilt for half a day.

Aunt Titia certainly noticed her gift quilt spread on the bed, but she made no comment until I spoke of it after we'd eaten and were having a smoke. She must know that it never served as cover; it was a memory quilt.

"I suppose every piece of those interesting old prints has a story," I remarked hopefully.

"Yes'm." She nodded. "Them old scrops is all full of ricollections."

"The prettiest is that piece your father brought you for a dress."

"Yes'm," she agreed. "Pappy allus knowed what 'as purty."

When we moved out to chairs on the porch, she sat pensive, her hands in her lap, absently fingering her worn gold signet ring.

"Them days and times," she began ("and I'hefted a piggin of anticipation"), "hit tuk seven to eight yards of goods fer a dress. I wore only narr' hoops. In the summer we had two cotton dresses fer a change, and in the wintertime two linsey fer the same reason. Them two linsey ud last two year, takin' 'em week about. A calica dress was quick made. The gals and women ginerally wore one linsey petticoat and over hit a thin white cotton petticoat, sometimes with ruffles.

"I remember jest like hit'as yestiddy the fust time I wore that dress...

"I'd made me a new bonnet. We done what you'd call notch plat the straw. This made a small bump ever' leetle ways. Rye straw was ginerally used 'cause hit bleached better'n wheat. We'd scald the straw to make hit soft, and when hit'as dry, we platted hit to make straw bonnets. Then we putt a colored band on 'em.

"Well, I had me a blue dress and a blue band on my bonnet. And I had new earrings. Them days and times you pierced yore ears with a needle. Then you run a silk thread through. They'd matter a leetle. Then when they warn't sore no more, you putt in the earrings. They'as common as screws are today."

She paused, dreamily remembering. Then she belched softly and resumed—

"I never wore a corset but onct. I'd made me this new calica dress with tight body and the skirt trimmed with ruffles. I thinks to myself, now I'll wear me a corset. That day we'as a-goin over to Uncle Samuel Lindsay's. So I putt on my corset that I paid fifty cents fer. Well, I got up on the hoss a-ridin' sidesaddle, and I thought to the land that corset ud cut my back in two. When I got over to Uncle Samuel's I went in the back room and pulled the gentleman off, and I hain't wore nary 'nother corset!"

"How old were you then?"

"I was fifteen year, ten month and sixteen days old."

"I'll bet you were pretty."

"I had nice hair. The plats was bigger'n yore arm, and way yonder long." She sighed. "Now my hair's so thin my head's might nigh naked. I have to keep hit tied up so's I'll not ketch cold. Yestiddy evenin' I pulled off me old headrag and was a-stirrin' about. This mornin' hit'as 'Ketchew!'" Cheerfully she resumed her story—

"And that day I wore my good shoes. They'as the last uns Pappy made fer me in quite a spell. Them days and times shoes fer the fam'ly was made by the father. The fam'ly'd kill a beef and have the hide tanned at the tanyard. And they'd share the meat. Nowadays, if'n a feller killed a beef, he'd be sich a hog he'd eat hit all hisself... or let it spile!"

My friend was a severe critic of modern life. The world's changes since her girlhood had not been for the better, to her way of thinking. Times may have been hard then; they were wicked now. People weren't neighborly like old, there was a heap more meanness, and too much drinking.

She continued—"Like I said, them was the last shoes Pappy made fer a while. And that'as the last time we had much of a getherin'. Fer the men all went off to the war, and the women was plumb frazzed a-tryin' to keep body and soul together. We had to work ever' endurin' minute. A-many a night atter the young uns was in bed, I've stole out and hoed corn by moonlight.

"Durin' war times ever'body helped. There warn't no men to do the work. Oh, they'as four white-headed and tottery old men, and they'd hobble along and sow the wheat. Then the women cut hit with reap hooks. The women couldn't cradle, hit'as too heavy fer 'em. So they used reap hooks, and somebody'd come behind 'em and tie the wheat. But I could cradle to the heels of any man.

"Then they'd build a leetle pen about a foot high with ten-foot rails laid acrost. They'd spread a sheet underneath that and flail the grain out. Then two women ud take the sheet and swing hit, and clean hit out purty as you please."

Life was hard for the women; it was hellish for the men. "Lord a mercy, I remember Pappy a-goin' off to war jest like hit'as yestiddy. He stayed three year. When he was wounded—I fergit the place—they sont him home. He was shot through the leg with a minie ball. And he had the diarrhee somethin' fierce when he come home. He got hit in the war. Sometimes fer days they'd go without a bite to eat. And sometimes fer days they'd go without a drink of water...

"The Confedrit soldiers didn't have much of any kind of uniform. Pappy said sometimes they had a piece of a par of shoes, and sometimes they went hit bar'foot.

Sometimes they had a whole par of britches, and sometimes they was plumb nigh naked. But they marched jest the same. And sometimes you could track 'em by the blood.

"Pappy wouldn't come in the house when he come home. Them days we had a big arn kittle at the spring where we done our washin'. Hit held forty gallon. Pappy told us young uns to fill hit up with water and build a far around hit. Then we should tote him some clo's out, but not putt 'em on the ground. He said to hang 'em on a limb.

"He got in the kittle and purt nigh scalded hisself. Then he picked up his old clo's and putt 'em on the far around the kittle. 'Fer,' he says, I've got lice on top of lice.'

"A bullet went through his leg and come out to the skin at the back. And the flesh was all tore off'n his thigh. But Mammy and me shore was glad to git him back any way atall. Pappy was eighty-nine year, six month and twenty-three days old when he died."

Making sorghum molasses

Appalachian Folks

Old Grist Mill

Chapter XV

Scarcely four months after he and I met in the school yard, Uncle Demon was sleeping under the weeds beside Dovey. In November the old man got an infected toe, and gangrene set in. "They cut off his leg below the knee," Tillie told me. "Then they had to cut it off again above his knee."

Aunt Titia pitied him. "Pore old feller, all by his lone. Disabled that-a-way he couldn't jest stay out'n the woods like a ridge rooter."

So she took him in. Besides, somebody else in the old house dwindled the clamor of her worrisome folks. Already she had taken care of three old people till they died. Her granmaw lived to ninety-one. There followed a feeble aunt of her pappy's. And he himself passed on when his daughter was sixty-eight years old.

Now came Demon, who surprisingly was no trouble at all.

"He didn't live but a leetle while," Aunt Titia said, stirring up gingerbread to celebrate my visit. "Twixt me and you, he purt' nigh starved to death of stinginess afore he come here."

"Probably," I said, "his meals were pretty much hit or miss."

"I reckon," she agreed. "Well, I never begredged him his vittles." She poured the batter into a kettle on the hearth. "Demon holp me a lot," she added generously." I've got a sight of wood blocked up out yonder that he sawed a-settin' in his cheer. And he'd peel taters fer me, or fruit when I made sass."

Coming to stay, Uncle Demon brought with him two things: a fairly new suit of clothes somebody had given him when he peddled roasting ears in town, and his coffin he made after Dovey went to her reward. Aunt Titia humored him and redd up a corner of her plunder room so he could sleep out there in the coffin, with his own pallet and some kivers made by his wife. That was what he wanted.

The arrangement worked well until one morning in late February when Aunt Titia found him dead. Now he had been gone two weeks.

"All he left behind was his hat and coat, and a par of hip britches," she said, busy making coffee. "One evenin' him and me was a-settin' by far, and Demon says, 'I cain't take these here britches with me, Tish, fer I'll go to Glory in my Sunday suit, but I want you to keep 'em.' I thought the old feller was plumb daft, but I give him promise." She giggled.

She turned out the gingerbread, then sank in her rocker to wait while it cooled. "Course," she went on, "old Demon's britches warn't hardly fittin' fer scournin' rags. But atter he'as gone, I figgered to keep my promise if'n I jest let 'em hang out in the plunder room. Then I felt somethin' hard in his pocket. Hit'as a wad of money. And my name was writ on hit!"

Then she remembered the day Demon asked her to write his name for him so he could see how it was going to look on his gravestone. She printed big letters. He studied them. Then he guessed maybe her name was longer than his. Humoring him, she wrote Titia Trail underneath. Now, in the back pocket of his hip britches she discovered the scrap of brown paper tied around the roll of bills. Demon Hately X (with curlicues) Titia Trail.

There wasn't all that much cash really. She figured the old man was hoarding it for more doctors and medicine, in case he had need. But he made out. So there it was. And after she had paid for his burying and set aside what was needed to letter his stone, she decided she could just keep the rest. For that was what Demon wanted.

Sundown on the Whittemore Branch

Chapter XVI

At Uncle Demon's funeral occasion they'd barely planted the old man before Aunt Titia had to face up to the perennial conflict of her wants and other's wishes. Various ones laid detaining hand on her—it was unthinkable that she should live all alone so far off from everybody. At her time of life she needed folks close by, they insisted, especially in the wintertime.

Although she acknowledged to herself that there was common sense in what they had to say, for she felt no surfeit of strength right then, still my friend didn't like the looks of common sense in that guise. The last thing she wanted on earth was jostling about in somebody else's household.

To avoid that, she made a fatal mistake, because her "rheumatiz was kinda actin' up right then," and insistence of others had her "fair whupped down." Against her better judgment, she took in an old couple needing a home. And from the first, they made her life miserable.

Circumstances surrounding the arrival of the Wises are vague in my mind because whenever Aunt Titia spoke of them she got snorting mad.

I saw the pair only once. In early May I drove out to Laurel Fork and stopped at the Trail place. The sight of three cars parked along the road gave me some anxious moments. But my fears were allayed when I hollered the house and Aunt Titia herself appeared in the doorway. She gave me no welcome. Her face was stony. At her back stood a couple of strange young men, one in a gray suit, the other in dark blue. In response to my sharp concern, she said flatly—

"No'm, I hain't sick. But come in."

I wanted only to leave, thinking this must be some momentous family council. And I half turned away, promising to return another time.

Whereupon, old man Wise edged through the crowded doorway as if he owned the place and smoothly explained that they were just about to have a little prayer. He invited me to join them, and was seconded by the stranger in gray. Aunt Titia, her face like a thundercloud, was given no opportunity to say anything. Though I declined his invitation, old man Wise refused to take no for answer. Either I rudely escaped or I must enter. Within, a third stranger stood waiting.

I accepted a "settin cheer" near the fireplace. Old man Wise, a meager elder with soupstrainer mustache and thin gray locks moistly combed over his bald spot, also took a straight chair. He crossed his legs, rested his elbow on one knee and bowed his forehead into the palm of his hand. His wife, a pinch-faced women with cold gray eyes and pious manner, knelt on the rag rug beside the spare bed. Aunt Titia eased herself down onto the second step of her attic stairs.

The three preachers stood in a row behind her long table which occupied the center of the room and was still burdened with the remains of a bounteous Sunday dinner. The individual in gray rested his fingertips on the tablecloth, closed his eyes, and began to pray in a clear firm voice.

He explained to the Lord that they were gathered here in this humble home on this beautiful day for the purpose of quiet communion together. He begged Him to bless this good man, a pillar of the church, and his faithful wife, the mother of fine, upstanding sons and daughters. "And bless this beloved old grandmother in the ripeness of her years who has guided so many faltering feet in the paths of righteousness," he entreated, working up to the holy tone.

Aunt Titia grimly stared straight before her.

The speaker thoughtfully invoked a blessing upon, "this beautiful young woman so miraculously sent" to be their welcome guest, urging the Father to guide her in the devine path to glory, "for the wages of sin is death." He wound up his pleading with an emphatic "Amen!," loudly echoed by old man Wise.

A slight pause, and the brother in blue took his turn beseeching in rolling tones, again bringing up "the wages of sin..."

Lastly, the third minister of the gospel, a horse-faced young man wearing thick eyeglasses, wafted heavenward his desires and requests, with no improvement in delivery over his fellows, and still doggedly concerned with the wages of sin.

Finally the whole long-winded petition was ended. Old lady Wise rose stiffly. Her man lifted his head and stood up to shake hands with the nearest preacher. Aunt Titia planted her stick squarely on the puncheons and got to her feet. She accepted the proffered hand of him in gray, with a perfunctory, "I'm glad to meet ye."

I made my escape.

Four weeks later when I returned, the Wises were gone, leaving behind great bitterness. At the mere mention of their name, Aunt Titia's ire all but choked her.

"I had me own old hut and my nastiness piled in hit," she fumed. "I didn't want nobody a-pilferin' around my things."

She was outraged by the unflagging efforts of old lady Wise (on whose conscience my friend's sins evidently weighed heavily) at bringing her salvation.

I asked, "Where did she find so many preachers?"

"Oh, they'as some kind of protracted meetin' a-goin' on."

"I like the music at revival meetings," I said.

Aunt Titia snorted. "Oh, they sing like a passel of catbirds down at the church. You never hear the old hymns no more. You could take all the religion they've got down there and tie hit up in a rag to a flea's leg, and *then* hit ud jump a quarter and bite ye!"

Aggravations with the Wises were constantly "nerve-frazzlin."

Their snappish little old feist had been a trial. He fancied Aunt Titia's cushioned chair by the fire. And he gave Becky cat no peace. But the crowning insult was one day finding the dog asleep in her bed.

"Nobody could tetch him," she said. "Pint yore finger at him and he'd bite ye. I never said nothin'. I jest went outside and cut me a nice strong hick'ry. Then I come into the room with hit behind my back. And when I got to the bed, I come down with hit as hard as I could, clost enough so's he felt the breeze. Let me tell you, he come out of there a-flyin'."

Him being in her bed at all she blamed on Miz Wise, because the dog was too short in the legs to climb up there all by himself. "Old lady Wise was a mean un," she declared vehemently, "and not bold mean, nuther. She was sneakin' mean."

And meddlesome. And grasping.

"One day Tillie sont me a couple of leetle white chickens. Old lady Wise says they'as both pullets; she'd take one I'd take t'other'n. I told she take nary un!"

No wonder him and her had been knocking about the world with no home of their own. They were both too trifling to live.

"That old man—he'as so pokey slow he couldn't ketch a cricket, and hit a cripple. I jest wanted to give him a dose of fishhooks in his rations. I reckon I could go to jail and fight lice and eat cowpeas if'n I had to...

"One day I was a-goin' to hoe my corn. Old man Wise said he'd hoe hit. I said I didn't mind hoein' hit. But he said he would. So I set in my cheer. I'd ketched a leetle cold. He went on off. The next time I seed my gyarden, the briars was growed up and a-bloomin'!"

There was no privacy anymore. Visits with her friends became pleasures of the past. If company came, old lady Wise scrouged right in. The day one of the schoolteachers stopped by and inquired about a granddaughter now married, Aunt Titia got down her box of pictures to show off the newest baby. Out fluttered Miz Wise with her box of snapshots and she had to tell all about everyone. "Nobody keered a bit in this world about them old fuzzy pitchers of her'n." My friend glowered even in the telling. "I felt like wringin' her skinny neck."

With them underfoot, Aunt Titia got so hornety she could hardly live with herself. "They was times," she admitted, "that old lady Wise riled me so, if'n I'd a-had the stren'th, I'd a-flang a pot at her."

Somebody sent up a jar of spiced beans, and Miz Wise took it. "She says, 'I reckon we'll eat these fer dinner.' I says, '*I*'ll eat the beans, and you'ns can smell of the plate!'"

Chafing under the daily grind with these trashy people she so wholeheartly despised, Aunt Titia, as she sat "glumin' by the far," about decided that the only way she could get rid of them was to go herself. "I was in sich a powerful pucker to git shet of 'em, I reckon I'd a-gone down to Em's," she confessed with a little grimace, "where the bedbugs tries to claim kin." She chuckled. "Seem like the bugs don't bother Em none, but I'm a fresh mess in, and they jest help theirselves."

But it happened that Aunt Titia just flew mad and ordered them off the place. "That mornin'," she related, "I ketched old lady Wise a-pilferin' in my things. Said she's a-lookin' fer the tablecloth. Well, I'd done hid hit. Her and me had a tilt. I says to her, I says, 'Now you'ns jest pack up yore plunder and git out. Go cadge some'eres else.'

"She commence to moan and carry on about how they didn't have no place to go. I says, 'You can jest hunt up somebody else that's largehearted.' I says, 'You got all day fer hit, and I'll not have you'ns under my roof nary 'nother night.'

"I didn't tarry a-listen' to her flareback. I went out to the spring fer a fresh print of butter. And when I come back I heerd Miz Wise a-whagin' things around in the house.

"They went off a-totin' their bags and boxes, and their leetle feist was a-trotin' at their heels. Old lady Wise kep' a-moanin' about no place to lay their heads. But right then I didn't have no feller-feelin'."

Nor was she more kindly disposed when she had assessed the cost of their stay—"They jest stripped me. I heerd tell that she's dead now. I reckon she's a-totin' chunks fer Somebody. They tuk my corn, and my kerosene jug. And I had a par of leetle side combs. I cain't find 'em high new low. She said they'as purty."

Aunt Titia peered at a burly fellow walking up the road. He had come to do some work for her. As he spoke and continued on around the house, she excused herself and went back to tell him what she wanted done. Becky cat showed up to keep me company.

"Twixt me and you," Aunt Titia resumed as she settled back in her chair, "I never drempt I'd git shet of them trashy people so easy. I had orta pinted out the road to 'em afore I done hit. Pappy allus said, 'twarn't wuth while to whup the Old Boy around the stump; jest give him a lick over hit."

"But I'd been feelin' sorta feeblish, and I was aimin' to putt up with 'em ontil I kindly got my stren'th back. That day, though, I'as so mad I didn't keer about nothin'.

"And soon's them two left out, hit'as jest like a big sack off'n my shoulders. Seem like I couldn't wait to git the stink of 'em out'n the house. I jest tore up the patch. I hung the kivers out to sun and air. I washed up and swep' the floor, and putt the furniture back where it belonged. The clods was a-flyin' ever' which-a-way." She chuckled. "Then I got a ketch in my back, and I warn't wuth shucks the rest of the day."

So, pouring herself a cup of coffee, she rested. And the peace there in her old house was sweet as a sugar candy—just her old clock ticking and the birds chirping up in a corner of the attic. Feeble or not, hereafter she'd go it alone. Freedom was so sweet. No more listening to that jimberjawed old women. "Ner him a-snorin'. I tell you, that old man could shore rattle the rafters. I got so easy in my mind a-settin' there in me old cheer that I drapped off to sleep. And Becky she woken me when she come a-sneakin' in, spyin' this way and that fer the leetle old feist."

A warm poultice eased her back and the quiet of the house soothed her spirits. With satisfaction she resumed her old comfortable habits. She ate a peaceful supper, then took up her reading.

But she was not through with the Wises yet. And near about bedtime she flew mad again. "I'm a-settin' there a-readin' a new book I'd kep' hid in me old featherbed," she said, boiling with indignation. "And jest as I git to the excitin' part, my lamp weaks down and goes out."

That was when she discovered they had taken her kerosene jug. Eleven o'clock at night, and nary a drop of oil on the place!

She couldn't do more than fumble her way into bed. But the night's rest made her feel better. She awoke with the first twitterings of the birds, wondering what time it was. And when the clock struck five she decided not to bed it any longer.

Her face washed in what little "dead" water was left in the bucket, she combed her hair, noticing how the wad of combings, thrown in the fire, sizzled up, loud in the quiet. Going to the spring, she thought Heaven must be like that morning, it was so fair. And after her breakfast, which she relished to the last bite, she took hoe in hand to the garden. Becky dallied along too, looking and listening for mice in the weed patches.

After about an hour's hoeing, slow and easy, she set a spell.

"John he come," she gave me a sideways grin, "and there I was—jest as happy as a pig in the sunshine."

Abandoned log cabin

Chapter XVII

But Aunt Titia's newfound bliss proved all to brief. And she had only herself to blame. She started in from the garden to meet us when Tillie and I stopped by, and we saw her fall. We both went running.

From tags left on the fence she realized that somebody had stolen bedclothes she forgot and left out all night. "I got so riled," she told us, "I never looked where I'as a-steppin'. A big old briar ketched aholt of my apern, and there I drawed my pitcher on the ground."

We had lifted her out of the garden dirt. Miraculously no bones seemed to be broken, and we helped her to the house. But she kept stewing. "If'n I'm a-gonta steal, I'll not steal bedclo's and sichlike as that," she fumed. "I'll steal me a leetle bite to eat. And I'll not wait till I git too hongry to tote a load nuther!"

Tillie said quietly, "They could come and carry *you* off up here, and you'd never know it."

"I wouldn't onless they pinched me," Aunt Titia admitted with surprising candor. "If'n I lay on this ear," she tapped a forefinger against her right temple, "I cain't hear nothin'. They could come in and walk all around, and I'd not hear 'em."

"Well," Tillie answered reasonably, "you'd want to be peart enough to put up a good fight, jest in case. Gettin' over yore fall, I reckon you'll find a bruise or two, and maybe some stiffness. Whyn't you come home with me fer overnight. It's Clyde's birthday, and I was aimin' to fix cake and grapejuice."

To our surprise, Aunt Titia was agreeable. Little did we dream as they stifled the fire and fastened the door behind them that she would be so long returning. She'd had a real jolt, and for a while was stiffer than common. Then, she thought she must have had something like pneumonie fever that kept her laid up a spell at Tillie's.

That's where I next saw her when I stopped by with only a few minutes to spare. It was what she called a sour day—unseasonably cold and wet, and her face was no sunnier than the weather. She still felt "drug out," and she had a corn that gave her twinges. "I've got a toe I'd like to trade ye," she offered with her quavery laugh.

In a little armless rocker she hugged the fire and lent her lap to sewing. Orange light wavered on the dark ceiling and spread in a pool over the hearthstone, caressing her old hands and glinting on her needle. Her face was flushed from the heat, which made her glasses so hot that from time to time she had to remove them.

"I'll git my piddlin' box," her smile was wan. "I want to show you my leetle piddlin' doin's."

She had been piecing a quilt from the most minute scraps of gigham—tiny inch squares of solid colors combined with small diamonds and triangles of figured materials. "I have to have my leetle bit of work," was her excuse for such painstaking labor. "I told 'em I'as aimin' to call hit 'Joseph's Coat'. Hit had many colors." The back of the quilt would be made from pokes tobacco came in; there was a big stack saved, washed up and ready.

She turned the pile of finished pieces over on her knee. "If'n I live till tomorrer, and hit's a day fit, I'm a-goin' to count", she said. "I had one hundert and twenty-three squar's last count... Hit uster be I didn't have so much time to make quilts. That'as mostly what I done to enjoy myself. Nowadays, I cain't do nothin' much else. And my mind hain't like a sheep jumpin' a fence, if'n I'm a-quiltin'."

The fire snapped and hissed over the rusty andirons. Aunt Titia sat with her skirts hoisted above the strip of calico that held up her yarn stockings where they met her long underwear. "You'll have to excuse me," she said. "I hain't laced up my shoes 'cause some days the strings hurt my ankles." She gave me a weak smile. "I hain't shed my underwear yet, but I'm aimin' to. mebbe next week."

She placed her piddling box on the seat of a chair at her elbow, with her little scissors on top. The scissors had belonged to her old granmaw. "I throwed 'em in the far yestiddy," she said. "I had some scrops in my lap. They called me to dinner and I got up. When I come back I couldn't find 'em. Tillie went to poke the far up and found 'em in the ashes, red hot.

Absently she fingered a slit in her apron where she had cut it along with a quilt scrap. "I jest hain't wuth shucks," she said, disgusted. "And the sight of me in this old raggedy dress...But I reckon nobody I know could tell the difference in a b'ar fight."

I left her utterly depressed.

Only a couple of weeks later, her spirits were sky high. She was back in her cabin. Somewhat. Tillie let her drive the mule and buggy over to spend the day any time she was a mind to.

That morning she had hoed corn awhile but had to quit on account of a light rain shower. She was resting in her old rocker on the porch, her misshapen straw hat hung on one knob back of her head, hands folded in her lap and her gaze afar in the mountains where the mists smoked. A rain frog was crooning out under her big oak tree.

Recognizing me, she giggled like a schoolgirl. "Now who in the world ud think the rain ud bring you! Come in and set a spell."

She had to admit that at Tillie's she was fairly well satisfied. She did as she pleased. And she liked children. Still—"That fam'ly's a mite too birthy fer me," she confessed with a half-guilty laugh. "They's sich a passel of young uns there, and they raise sich ructions...Tillie's all heart, bless her. But she's sorta like a women I uster know—she'd be a-hippin' one and expectin' another'n."

She harked back to her troubles with the Wises. "Nobody knows what I suffered with them trashy people." Her expression was doleful. "And I'm a way behind with my garden. But Tillie made one of the boys keep hit clean while I was laid up. Oh, I've got an awful crap out yonder." She laughed. "Four rows of corn, two rows of beans, one of 'maters and two of taters...

"And I'm a-gonna make some jelly. But I cain't build a far till my leetle birds gits out'n the nest. They's a chimney sweeper's nest with three leetle birds in hit. And they sweep the sut down suthin' awful."

Though her hearth was cold, she kept her clock running. And when it had wheezed through twelve hasty strokes, she got up to collect her dinner. I sat by to visit, having lunched early. She lifted the cloth from her table. Into a tall jelly glass she dippered fresh water. Then she munched cold boiled potato, lettuce chopped up, a piece of fried fish with onion, and some leftover biscuit. To top off, she pulled towards her a glass of fox grape jelly, helped herself to a couple of spoonsful, then replaced the newspaper cap, firmly tying the string that held it in place.

All the while, the birds' twittering reminded us of their busy family life in her chimney.

"This hain't a good year fer cherries," Aunt Titia remarked between puffs on her wee pipe. "That leetle blue snow in April ruint 'em. And them leetle blue violets in the woods—I jest love 'em might nigh better'n anything—we didn't have none of them this year."

"What's a blue snow?" I asked.

"A blue snow? You know when the snow is big and fluffed up and falls right heavy, hit piles up in no time, and ever'thing's right still—hit ain't cold. But one of them snows that jest whizzes and fizzes, with leetle bitty fine flakes, hit's so cold you cain't stand hit hardly. They can be jest a leetle bit of snow on the ground, and hit's jest freezin' cold. That's a blue snow. The air is blue."

A lean hound looked in at her upper door. Aunt Titia gave him a plate of scraps that he gobbled up. "He come here one day last week," she said. "Putts me in mind of an old dog I uster have. Hub was his name. And he was the masterfulest dog fer huntin' ever I seed. Of a night I'd hear him off som'eres. I'd git me up out of bed, putt on my clo's, and take me a torchpine and light hit, and I'd go atter my dog. If'n the possum was up a sablin', I'd shake him down. Old Hub ud never take his eyes off'n that possum. He'd grab him by the neck, look up at me, and start fer home with him."

She laid up her pipe and glanced about the room.

"Lord a mercy, I've got sich a wilderness of things to do. While I'as gone, and no far in the house, the j'ists got all mildewed." And without Becky around (she was still at Tillie's), the mice found her dresser drawers. They wounded an old, old rag doll she was keeping. "The only boughten doll I ever had was about this long." She measured half way up her forearm. "Hit's head was jest small, with black hair. But I never got time to play with hit. And Em, when she'as a leetle youngun, she played with hit and broke hit. This'n's one Granmaw made fer me." Dollie had great character but she looked sad.

And the mice gnawed the fringe off her best tablecloth that was sixty or seventy years old. "Mammy had hit," she said. "We kep' hit fer comp'ny. But old lady Wise rooted around till she found hit and she putt hit away dirty. Hit's white linen with a red border. They made the wust mess."

"Did you set a trap?" I asked.

"I putt some medicine out fer 'em." She spoke grimly. "I had some of this what they call nux vomikie. They say hit kills ary thing that's born with hits eyes shet. I uster putt hit in my chicken feed. Then if'n a hawk ketched 'em, hit ud kill the hawk but wouldn't bother the chickens. The mice jest et hit up, and I hain't seed so many of 'em since."

She laid a cloth over her plate which she would wash in hot water at Tillie's. "Let's me and you go set on the porch," she said, "and have us a good chat."

We went outside, but she'd scarcely sunk into her chair when she snapped her fingers and bounced up again. She laughed, "As Pappy uster say, what brains you don't have in yore head, you got to have in yore heels."

From indoors she fetched a brown paper poke out of which she took her handwork, re-wound the loose yarn on the ball, and resumed knitting a sock with wooden needles. She had carded the wool, spun the thread, dyed it an unfading blue, and made up what she called her "pulley ball". This was yarn so wound that one thread could be pulled from the center, while the other came off the outside, and the two socks were knitted from equal lengths of the same thread.

A light shower passed, barely penetrating the thick foliage of her big oak. Aunt Titia glanced up into the branches above where the rain frog piped his tune. "I jest love me old tree," she said. "I hope hit keeps on a-growin' till the end of time." She scrutinized her last row of stitches, then went on—

"A while back, a feller come by and he says, 'I'll trim yore tree afore the sap comes up next year fer the farwood.' I says, 'You'll do nothin' of the kind.' I says, 'I reckon nature'll trim hit.'

"Pappy set sich store by the old tree. He uster say, "Hit's got the best balanced top ever I seed.' I ricollect one night afore he died, hit come a storm of wind. The akerns was like hail on the roof. Pappy said he wanted me allus to take keer of the old tree. 'If'n the Almighty sees fit to blow hit down,' he says, 'that's all right. But don't you never let nobody cut hit down.' He says 'Trees like this'n hain't growed in a day ner a month ner a year.'

"I says, 'I can drag or tote my wood, Pappy.'"

Chapter XVIII

Pushing open her cabin door, Aunt Titia listened for the twittering of the chimney swifts and met only big silence. The nest was empty at last! From that moment, she was in swivet to move back home.

Without hearth fire, the heart of the house had been dead. But life revived when flames again forked up the chimney and my little old friend contentedly puttered about.

It seemed like the good old times that morning I rode over and looked down upon the cabin caught in a shoot of sunshine with smoke rising from its chimney clutched in creeper.

I cut quite a figure, riding up, so that Aunt Titia had a laughing fit. For I sat astride a tired old work horse lent me for his keep. He was a big, rawboned, salt-and-pepper animal named Fred. His spavined leg made speedy travel a bit rocky, but he had an easy walk that permitted leisurely viewing of the countryside.

"I tell you," Aunt Titia controlled her mirth, "if'n I could go back forty year, I'd have me a hoss afore Sat'day night."

"You like horses?"

"Yes'm. I was might nigh raised on a hoss. I reckon I was five year old when I fust rode a hoss. And I went to mill when I warn't big enough to hold the sack on. Pappy tied hit on, and I'd hop me up a-straddle the hoss."

My friend had sent word for me to come and eat dinner with her. The beans were washed and ready for the pot, with a smidgen of fatback. She peeled the potatoes while we sat on the porch.

I was anxious to hear how she made out the night before, because a violent thunderstorm had rampaged over the mountains. But I could have saved my worry.

"I jest stretched out in me own old bed," she said smugly, "and hit a-rainin'. I laid there and watched the pinky lightnin' a-winkin' at the winders and through the cat-hole in the door."

Already she had plans for making a sight of jelly. Besides a few huckleberries yet, in another week, about, the blackberries would be ripe. She had started. But her wrist was tied up. "A harnet ketchin' flies sot down and stung me when I'as a-makin' my apple momalade," she said.

Flicking her eyes over Fred, tied in the shade, his head hanging and his tail switching, she let her thoughts range back across the years to her pet of long ago. "I remember jest as well as if hit'as yestiddy when Kirk's army come," she began pensively. "Mammy and me was out in the field cuttin' a passel of grass fer the hoss.

"We had the sweetest leetle old mare you'd ever want to see. We called her Sally. And oh, I could jest ride her anywheres. She'd come to me and putt her head down fer me to putt the bridle on. Then she'd walk up to a stump and wait fer me to git on her. Sometimes I'd stand on a stump and make Sally run by, and I'd hit her ever' time. And don't you think I didn't make her go under me. I jest loved her.

Appalachian Folks

"When we got to the house, Mammy told me to go back down in the field and fetch another armful of grass. I went out to the field, and after I'd got the grass I come back acrost the road and clim a bank.

"Jest then I heerd a tremenjous racket. I looked up the road and I seed the men come a-ridin'. They had Sally, and she was jest a-dancin'.

"I never moved. I jest stood right there on the bank with my armful of grass hugged to me. Oh, I'as so mad. I didn't keer fer nothin'. I looked the leader right squar' in the eye and I says—

"'You low-down, triflin' pup, you tuk my hoss.'

"He says, 'Hit's no business of yore'n.'

"I says, 'Hit is, or I wouldn't be a-mindin' hit.' I says, 'My mammy's a lone woman with five little children, and we need our hoss.'

"He jest laughed and rode on."

"When I come in the house, I says to Mammy, 'They tuk Sally.'

"She says, 'I know they did. But now I think, I hain't right shore, but I think they left another'n in the stable. Run out yonder and see if hit's dead. If hit ain't, see if hit can hold hit's head up. And feed hit some grass.'

"I says, 'Well, hit'll die, fer I hain't a-goin' to feed hit.' Oh, I'as so mad. Hit'as a big bony old thing, they'as big sores on hits back. I says, 'If'n yo're alive, raise yore head up, and if'n yo're dead, jest lay where you air.'

"Mammy come up behin' me and she says, 'What air you a-mutterin' about?'

"I says, 'Hit'll die shore, and me and you cain't drag hit out of the stable.'

"But hit riz up hits head. Mammy says, 'Putt the grass down fer hit.'

"That evenin' Old Uncle Rufe come over and I says, 'Uncle Rufe, you orta see the purty thing we've got in the stable.'

"He says, 'Why honey, what is hit?'

"I says, 'Hit as nigh' nothin' as you'd wanter see.' I says, 'Hit'll not live nary 'nother day.'

"He went out to look at hit, and he says, 'Hit'll live. Tomorrer,' he says, 'I'll fetch over some things and wash hits back.'

"And shore enough, next mornin' hit'as on hits feet. We named hit June. And hit'as a good hoss.

"The army tuk ever'body's hoss. They tuk old Uncle Pete's. And they tuk Aunt Martha's. And old Uncle Clint had two. They tuk both of his'n.

"That night I didn't git a wink of sleep fer frettin' about Sally. So next mornin' I lit out and walked down to whur the soldiers was camped in the fields. I went to the Captain and I says, 'I come to git my hoss.'

"They was hunderts of hosses all around. He says, 'You cain't find yore hoss.'

"I says, 'Yes, I can.'

"He was a-tryin' to keep from laughin'. But he says, 'If'n you can find yore hoss, you can have hit.'

"I says, 'I aim to ride her home.'"

"We went out to where the hosses was, and I sung out, 'Sallee—if'n you hear me, nicker.' And Sally nickered. Oh, she come up to me and rubbed her nose all over me and nudged my arm.

"The Captain says, 'I don't believe she's yore hoss.'

"So I left her and went in amongst the other'ns and sung out, 'Sallee—nicker!'

"And Sally nickered agin.

"The Captain says, 'All right. You can have yore hoss.'"

Cabin on Whittemore Branch

Mr. and Mrs. Reeves of Leicester, NC

Chapter XIX

It had been several years since I stopped by the working mill on Carver's Creek where one could buy for ten cents a poke of water-ground meal still warm from the grinding. I remembered a ramshackle building that shuddered under the thunderous pounding of the big wheel. Cold, sparkling water poured down through the flume, spilling wastefully over wet rocks inhabited by green crayfish. Inside, cobwebs hung thickly from the beams, all hoary with cornmeal dust, and great barrels of white corn stood in the dimness. Now that I felt some "romantic involvement" with Uncle Jonny Lindsay, I went back for more than a little poke of meal.

I found the old gentleman that morning out swapping talk with a customer whose saddled horse, a chunky claybank, was tied to the fence nearby. They sat together in the thin shade of a cluster of saplings beside a row of mailboxes, on a great puncheon log seat convenient for folks awaiting the postman. At their feet lay a brown shepherd dog.

Uncle Jonny and the dog rose and came to meet me. He was a fine figure of a man, very tall, and he walked erect with spring to his step. His short beard grew full and snow-white like his hair curling along his shirt collar, but his dark eyes were sharp and twinkling. Doffing his straw hat in a very courtly manner, he gave me a firm handshake. The dog gently wagged his plumy tail, and I patted the top of his head.

"Shep's gittin' old and pettish," Uncle Jonny said. "He jest loves to be petted."

My reception was perhaps especially cordial, since he remembered my father having fitted his wife a pair of glasses. But as I spoke of buying some cornmeal, he shook his head. "When the water gits low," he said, "the corn's skeerce fer sellin'. Times I've got a-plenty water, I can grind fifteen or twenty bushel of corn a day. But this way hit takes all day to grind a trifle."

The stream was thin, yet much of that trickle was lost, spilling through rotted timbers. For the old man hesitated to climb high places. "You'll notice the building's a-goin' to wrack," he mourned. "But cain't do much about hit. Whenever I climb up now, I git drunk and could easy fall."

Still, the old wheel slowly turned with rattle and grind, and inside the dim building the grains of corn kept up a shuffle and dance, while snowy meal sifted down to form a soft little pyramid.

Time's changes left Uncle Jonny sad. "There's been a mill here, some kinda mill," he remarked, "ever since I was jest a chunk of a kid. And I'm ninety, soon be ninety-one, year old. First there was a sawmill here; then my daddy putt up a grain mill. Olden times hit tuk six days a week and about three nights to keep up with the grindin'. But the way hit is now, a man that could do eight hours of work a day couldn't afford to fool with hit. Sometimes I git a gallon and a half, sometimes I git a peck. The way the water is, no wonder I look tacky and all."

But I thought he looked mighty fine. His light blue shirt, its soft collar fastened by a brass collar button, had been neatly ironed; and his dark gray pants, loosely held to his waistline by suspenders lightly draped over his shoulders, looked practically brand new.

I carried my camera, and I asked him for his picture in front of the mill. "It's a very good camera," I assured him.

"Oh, I don't doubt hit takes good pitchers," he returned. "That's is, if there's anything good in front of hit."

Then he told a story himself, of another picture taking. A couple of artists were at the mill painting pictures. A child wandered by. She and Uncle Jonny, with old Shep, stood awhile in the doorway watching the painter at work inside. They forgot about the other fellow busy outside, until he called them over and showed them where he had painted them, and the dog too, peeping in the door.

The customer still waited on the puncheon seat. Now I saw under his straw hat the genial face of John Trail. We nodded recognition.

Uncle Jonny was loath to see me go. He thought we ought to set a spell and talk over our folks; he had a notion that we might be related, since his grandmother's family had the same name. He said gallantly, "I allus like to claim kin with good-lookin' women."

John Trail reminded him that he should beware of women.

But Uncle Jonny retorted, "Some of the men are sorta tricksy too."

The other was disposed to jolly him—"What you mean, an old relic like you, a-spillin' pitchers?"

"Oh, I don't know you, and I don't wanter," Uncle Jonny joked, turning his back. "The idear, him callin' *me* an old relic!"

A freckled barefoot boy came down the road. And a grizzled countryman rode in bareback on a mule. The mailman drove up. I thought this gave me an excuse to leave. But Uncle Jonny was unwilling still.

"Set awhile," he urged, "and we'll go up to the house and bust a tater. I'm not foolish about taters, but a tater bustin's the thing about dinner time."

I declined. And so I never met his wife. Aunt Caroline died suddenly towards the end of October.

Chapter XX

Near noontime of her eighty-sixth birthday, I stopped by Aunt Titia's to leave her a little present. She was especially fond of canned pineapple, and I had brought some of the fruit candied as well.

Misting rain kept her on the porch, with a lap full of sewing. "I'm a-patchin' a quilt linin'," she announced. "Come a cold night, you'd no keer if'n hit *was* patched."

With her sat Melissie, the favorite granchild, whom I met now for the first time. Though in her mid-twenties, the girl looked much younger, being small of person with delicate features. Her face and slender hands were sun-tanned, her hair was dark brown, her eyes honey-colored. Quietly she sat on the edge of the porch, leaning against a post "to keep her back straight," her granny explained.

Aunt Titia's mood was lighthearted and gay. Side-stepping a celebration so's not to hurt anybody's feelings hadn't been easy. "But I putt 'em off," she gloated. "I says to 'em, wait until I'm ninety year old. Then we'll have the biggest shindy ever seed in these parts." Her amusement betrayed a conviction that she would not likely have to fulfill that promise.

Well-wishers aside, she prepared to enjoy her day the way *she* wanted. To begin with, there was the duck egg she had the promise of. 'They's a feller over at the head of Carver," she had mentioned earlier, "that's got up'ards of thirty ducks. One day he come past, and I says to him, 'If'n you don't do nothin' else,' I says, 'I want you to fetch me a duck egg fer my breakfast on my birthday.' He says, 'If'n you live till the twenty-third day of July, you shall have hit.'"

He was as good as his word. "He brung me two," she said. And luckily he did, for it gave her one extra to share with an unexpected visitor—"Afore seven o'clock this mornin' I heerd somebody holler the house, and my cousin, Obie Trail, come up on the porch. He says, 'Wal, Tish, I tuk my foot in my hand and come over to set a spell with ye on *our* birthday. Only the good Lord knows if'n we'll see another'n.'

"Well, he come on in, and him and me et the duck eggs. Obie'd got a soon start and walked over from his place. He lives about six mile t'other side the mountain. He's eighty-eight year old today, and mighty peart fer his age. I shore was proud to see the old feller."

I said, "I'm sorry I couldn't meet him."

"He stayed only jest about an hour, fer he was aimin' to stop at one or two other places. But me and you could go over and see him some day. You'd like Obie. He's a droll-natured feller.

"I remember jest like hit'as yestiddy one Sunday we all went to preachin'. In front of Obie was a-settin an old feller and he'as called on to pray. He got down right this-a-way," she cupped her hand over her mouth and wriggled her face, "tuk a cood of terbaccer out'n his mouth, laid hit on the bench aside of him and laid his hat over hit.

"While he'as a-prayin', Obie got all the coods of the men a-settin' near abouts and putt 'em under the hat.

"The old feller said, 'Amen!', retched under his hat fer his terbaccer and tried to putt hit in his mouth. Hit'as way yonder too big. He says, 'That's the fust time I ever knowed terbaccer to swell.'

"Obie says, 'Hit does sometimes.' He never let on."

I laughed. Melissie smiled shyly. Aunt Titia took about six running stitches on the quilt lining, and paused again.

"A-many's the time durin' preachin' when I wished I'as out where I could take me a good hearty laugh," she went on. "I had to bite my lip or cram my hankercher in my mouth to keep from laughin' in church.

"Another time, I ricollect, when me and Tempe went to meetin', our cousin Jonny wanted to set atween us. There was an older gal named Caroline Davis in front of him. She was all dressed up, a-wearin' a bustle, and hit rested on his knees.

"Durin' preachin' he leant over to me and says, 'I'm a-goin' to stick my knife in that thing.'

"I says, 'Don't you dar'!'

"He says, 'Yes, I am. Hit's a-wearin' out my knees.' And he says to Tempe, 'I'm a-goin' to stick my knife in that thing.'

"She says, 'Don't you dar', Jonny Lindsay!'

"Well, the preachin' went on. And about the time hit'as through I seed the wheat bran a-spillin' out of that bustle. And when she got up to walk, hit jest kep' a-spillin' out behind her. She'd filled a poke with wheat bran.

"Jonny says, 'I'll bet she walks a lot lighter now!'"

Aunt Titia's old clock wheezed through twelve quick strokes. She laid aside her sewing. Melissie had come to eat dinner with her. And later on, Tillie would be over for fresh gingerbread. She invited me to stay for a little snack, but I had to meet an appointment. And I would be away for several weeks, going to Chicago.

My friend didn't envy me. One taste of city life when she was asked to participate in the State Fair was all she could stomach. "I like fur back," she reiterated. "I like God's nature as He made hit."

"Well," I said, "the sooner I go, the sooner I'll get back to God's country."

"Don't stay away too long now," she begged. "I moughtn't be here when you git back." She scratched her elbow and noticed the frayed sleeve of her calico waist. "This old raggedy dress..." she said with her quavery laugh. "If'n the rag man comes by yore place, don't tell him where I am."

The fact was, Tillie had made her a new dress for her birthday. And she planned to get all "primpted up" that evening. Only the fabric would be new; her dress style never changed. She preferred a long-sleeved, front-buttoned waist with plain neckband usually fastened by a safety-pin, and long full-gathered skirt hemmed around her shoetops. Gray was the color.

Melissie'd had nothing to say. And she never willingly met my glance. If surprised studying my face, she smiled shyly and looked away. Aunt Titia had remarked with some regret the uncommon reserve of her favorite. For Melissie was not backward. As a child she loved to go to school and she was unusually bright in her studies. But when she was fourteen and in the seventh grade, her mother took sick and Melissie had to give up the classroom for drudgery at home.

By the time she could go back to school, she was twenty, and too old. She got married. Now she had a little boy almost five.

Old Grist Mill

Appalachian Folks

"Snake Man's" cabin, Uncle Samuel Crisson, State Hwy #19: Marion to Spruce Pine near Hollisfield, NC

Chapter XXI

August was well along before I met Aunt Titia again.

"Now who in the world ud be a-lookin' fer you?" Her blue eyes sparkled with her welcoming smile. "I'm mighty proud to see ye. Come in and set a spell."

She took her short-legged chair that hugged her like it was molded to an exact fit, saying, "Last night shore was hot. I never shet my eyes till the clock struck twelve. I was all over the bed. I kicked and tossed and throwed the kiver off'n me."

"So this moring, hot or not," I scolded, "you got up and put out a big snowy wash. It dazzled me."

"My clo's couldn't help but be nice and white," she returned with modest pride. "I jest putt 'em in my leetle biler and bile 'em rale good, then I wash 'em with a-plenty good homemade soap (they's never no drags in my soap), and rench 'em off in runnin' water."

She fanned herself with the stiff brim of an old sunbonnet she picked off the back of her chair. In the oak the sawing of the jarflies waxed strong, faster and faster, then abruptly died away. With both hands she lifted the snowy tags of her back hair. "My bonnet tail was short," she laughed, "and the sun burnt my neck."

Except that her health had been good, her budget of news was all bad.

It seemed no matter how hard she worked, there was a discouragement about her gardening. "I bug my beans of a mornin'," she explained. "But there've been times when I thought I'd jest make out a deed and sign ever'thing over to the bugs. Same way with my maters and the worms. My sweet taters hain't doin' no good; the moles jest dig under ever'thing and ruint 'em."

Bad as this was, there had been a real serious happening. Her chimney fell down. "One sour evenin' me and Tillie was a-settin' by the far. She says, 'The chimley's a-goin' to fall.' I never moved. Hit'as jest a-pourin' the rain. Hit fell away from the house. But they'as a bumblebee's nest back in the chimley, and let me tell you, we come out of there. Hit rained the far out."

How her folks must have gloated over her misfortune! Now their contrary kinswoman would have to come down off her old lonesome mountain. They thought.

But Aunt Titia refused to budge even while the chimney was being rebuilt.

"I borried a stove," she recounted. " My apern was burnt, my fingers was burnt, a-tryin' to cook. When my chimley was fixed, and hit cost me better'n $200 to rebuild hit, I says, "Yer mammy's a-movin' home!" Fust meal I cooked, seem like hit'as the best. I love my farplace. I'd never no more fool with a cookstove. No, ma'am."

As fall came on that year, Aunt Titia was feeling fit and able to get her crops laid by. She had help with fodder pulling in the big field, and, after she tried it alone, with snaking in her firewood.

"I went out to git me a load of bresh," she said, "and I got so narvish I sweat jest like a hoss. I've got a pocket in my apern to tote my sweatrag in, but I'd left hit in the house; so I jest h'isted up my apern and wiped my face on hit."

After that, she arranged with one of Tillie's boys to take care of the heavy wood cutting. And before frost, her attic stair corner was stacked full of hearth logs.

For she paid attention to nature's signs and lived by them. Everywhere they foretold a severe winter. The cornshucks were thicker than common. One heard the thud of apples dropping until they lay in heaps under her gnarled old trees where yellow jackets sipped from split fruit. Another sign—the apples had tough skins. And there was a heavy crop of mast. Her old oak tree rained down acorns that fell at all hours, even in the still air, ripping through the leaves and striking her roof with a cracking thump.

So many warnings of rough weather ahead must rouse the prudent person to get ready. Aunt Titia kept pace with the hustle of the season. Her days were thronged. She dug taters, gathered cabbages, tied up her onions—"I'll jest hang 'em up," she said, "and they'll last me all winter 'thout rottin'. And when I want me an onionhead, I'll not have to borry hit. Ner beg!"

She made kraut to have the juice on hand for cough medicine. Fox grapes were put up to joy her sweet tooth. She stored her corn in the plunder room, and squirreled away some of the plentiful harvest of nuts. Early on, there was her share of delicious sourwood honey to be taken from the bee gums.

"My bees hain't never the least bit ill," she boasted, "'cause they know me. I'm around 'em all the time."

If thoughts of winter storms just over the horizon nagged her with forebodings, she never let on. At the height of autumn's glory, there came her very kind of day—very clear, very gay, and kind of sharp. And she climbed Old Baldy for one more breath-taking view of the whole round world.

When lowering skies sombered the naked woods and faded fields, and she was house-bound, *then* she could rest and be thankful.

Chapter XXII

Half way up the mountain, where the road curved sharply below a high bank on which a stone chimney rose starkly from a patch of weeds, I met a young lad walking down. He pointed to my car and yelled, "Flat tar!"

Sure enough. Willingly he loped off to bring help, while I waited.

Down toward the settlement a rig appeared, coming my way. An old white horse plodded up the hill, and a brown dog followed close behind.

Around the curve the thin iron-rimmed wheels grated on the gravel of the roadway. The horse caught sight of me beside my car and halted. The dog stopped, looked this way and that, then sat down to wait. On the buggy seat a man was huddled in his khaki-colored coat, his head covered by a huge cap with earflaps turned down, his knees protected from the damp cold by a faded bedquilt. Beside him lay a full plump grain sack and sundry brown paper pokes. He raised his eyes and lifted his white-bearded chin out of his coat collar. It was Uncle Jonny.

"Hello, Mr. Lindsay."

"Howdy, young lady." He greeted me kindly but there was sadness in his faint smile. "'Pears like trouble has overtuk ye."

"Well, yes. But help is on the way." I hoped my cheerful countenance would bring a flash of his wonted geniality.

But his face remained solemn. "Good," was all he said. Glancing up at the lowering sky, he added, "I'm afeared hit'll rain."

Clouds like smoke scudded overhead. The higher mountains were hooded in mists; the foothills rose dark and wet, little wispy clouds continually dissolving among their treetops. The wind had risen to a hollow roar in the pine woods. All at once darkness settled like premature nightfall, and there came the rustle of rain slanting across the slopes of broomsedge.

My tire fixer drove up, and Uncle Jonny clucked to his horse. "Well," he said, "I've got to git out'n the rain. I've got the influenzy." The wheels grated and old Shep rose to pad faithfully on.

The sight of them was saddening.

Tillie mentioned that Uncle Jonny hadn't been himself since Aunt Caroline died. "But then," she added, "him and her lived together a mighty long time. They was married something like sixty year, and she was livin' in his home a good while before that."

Kind soul that she was, Tillie worried considerably about Uncle Jonny left all by his lone. She tried to help him where she could. But nothing melted the gloom of his deep sorrow.

"Pore old gent." Her sympathy was boundless. "He acts about out of his mind. He don't even keep track of time no more. One of the cats after a mouse jumped to the mantelshelf and knocked the clock off, and all its innards got scrambled. Uncle Jonny jest tied up the case with a string and left it set."

She and I were on our way to buy a bedstead Uncle Jonny talked of selling. Rather than drive the long way around by the main road, she suggested that we walk over through the gap. "That way 'tain't far," she said.

Not far, but we had a stiff climb. Through the bars of various small fenced fields we toiled upward from the valley. Presently we entered a cattle trail that zigzagged through the woods up the steep flank of the mountain.

"It's cold as the north pole yonside this mountain," Tillie flung back at me as we walked single file. "This side the mountain is way yonder warmer than over where Uncle Jonny lives. I've seen it snow over there in November and lay on the ground till April. Over here it'll snow right heavy and pile up a foot or more in no time. Next day the sun comes out and it every bit melts away. On them mountains over yonder there'd still be snow."

The Jugtown potter and his family

From the gap, far reaches of lonely sky and wintry ridges opened before us. The only visible habitation in the wide panorama was the Lindsay home in the cove below. No sign of life appeared there.

But approaching the house we espied Uncle Jonny sitting on the porch, his stumpy chair tilted back against the log wall. Old Shep got up stiffly and came as far as the stepstones to greet us with a dignified wag of his plumy tail. The old gentleman was glad to see us, I felt, but his demeanor lost none of its joylessness.

Uncle Jonny took us through the big house which was shut up and dark. Wan daylight filtered down the black sooty throat of the chimney up which escaped a thin plume of smoke from a smoldering chunk. The place was neat, with the beds made and the dishes washed.

Jugtown Pottery buildings

In a small, narrow room added on, one tiny crooked window faced the door, and underneath it an old-fashioned sewing machine was pushed against the wall. On the machine lay a stack of quilt squares, with two pieces pinned under the presser foot. A handmade cord bedstead filled one whole end of the room, while opposite, quilted and woven bed covers were stored on open shelves.

I quickly bought the bed, and we passed again through the house. An unnatural quiet prevailed. Such sorrowing times left us uncomfortable.

"I tell you, hit's rough," Uncle Jonny said mournfully, with a slight gesture towards garments hanging on pegs against the wall. "When I come in here and see my folk's things, hit's rough. There's her coat and yonder hangs her hood that I tuk her to the hospital in...And she never got back. Hit's mighty lonesome, I tell ye."

"I know, Uncle Jonny," Tillie responded soothingly. "Whyn't you come stay with me fer a while, till you can get straightened out."

"Not now, I reckon," he answered gently. "But I thank ye."

Starting to climb the hill, we looked down to see the old man tipped back in his chair against the log wall with old Shep at his feet, exactly as we had found them.

Tillie's concern kept teasing her mind about what to do in the troubles of Uncle Jonny. "Seein' him so sorrowin' jest breaks my heart," she said. "Him that was always so kind and merry. Last winter when he turned ninety, he said, 'I've reached old age pint-blank to enjoy it.' And now, the way things are, he cain't."

She mused awhile, then added, "I reckon, though, he'll get over it, come time. Most everybody does. But losin' a dear soul you've lived with, friend and wife, fer more'n sixty year jest has to be rough, like Uncle Jonny says."

"Was Aunt Caroline related to Uncle Jonny?" I asked.

"No'm." Tillie bent to tie her shoelace. "But she lived in the family a good while before him and her was wed."

"Was she an orphan?"

"No'm. Her folks was all a-livin'."

We labored up a little stretch of steepness. It seemed that my quest for knowledge was not to be satisfied. But when we paused to catch our breath, Tillie gazed back down onto the Lindsay rooftree and explained. "Aunt Caroline was a Davis and they made up a right big family. But Uncle Jonny's mother took sick and dragged on fer years. They needed a girl—Uncle Jonny had jest one little brother that died, never no sisters—so they took in Aunt Caroline to look after the old lady. When she died, I reckon Uncle Jonny was so used to havin' Caroline around he jest up and married her."

"Did they have any children?"

"They had five girls. And outlived every one of 'em. Pore Uncle Jonny. All his fam'ly's layin' over in the buryin' ground. But I reckon he can be thankful he had Aunt Caroline as long as he did. She would be ninety-four, come Christmas. And she was a sweet, bright person right up to the end."

Chapter XXIII

Kinfolks told her she was crazy. Aunt Titia just laughed. "I told 'em I knowed that; tell me somethin' new."

Fault her however they might, her mind was set. "If'n I'm alive and able to move," she said firmly, "I'll be right here in me old house this winter. Whatever may happen can jest happen. I hain't a-goin' no place, and not nary 'nother pusson's a-comin' here."

"You act mighty spry," I told her. "Seems to me you get younger every year."

She grinned at me slantwise. "Well, I'll be truthful with ye, I'm kindly beginnin' to drag. but I'll pearten up when I git me some mistletoe." She cut a fresh-made apple upside-down cake to serve as a special treat for summer's end and my final departure that year. The day was dismal, but her lively hearth fire spread cheer and comfort. A cricket chirped by the chimney.

"Mistletoe?"

"Yes'm. Pappy allus said hit'as the best medicine in the world fer what ails old people. Last year one of the children fotched me a big bunch with a lavish of berries."

I said, "I thought mistletoe was just good for kissing under."

"That too," she assented. "And hit's fust-rate fer whatsoever ails ye if'n you have in mind to stay kissable."

She offered a crumb of cake to Becky who left her cushioned chair begging for more.

Since the sky was darkening down, and I had miles to cover, I took leave of my little old friend. From the porch she urged me to hurry back. And I promised, fervently hoping to find her there, "alive and able to move," in the little hut she loved so well.

Scarcely three weeks later, winter gripped her mountain early, in the teeth of a paralyzing blizzard...

"Fer weather," Aunt Titia recollected as we shared the porch on a balmy May morning, "that was a day to beat all. Hit commenced with a rainin', windin' spell, and fore bedtime come, drifty snow nigh kivered the fence out yonder."

Light broke darkly, through still air. All you heard were some crows caucusing over in the fields. The rain began pattering on the dead leaves, falling heavier by the minute till a downpour rapped on the roof and ran rivers around the house. The wind uprose, rocking the trees and lashing the rain against her log walls.

At noontime, when she looked out her door, it was spitting snow. Sleety fine flakes already rimed her doorstones and the yard grass.

Bethinking she ought to fill her water bucket before traveling got bad, she jammed on a battered felt hat over her headrag and buttoned on her heavy man's coat. Lard pail in hand, she took the path springward. Careful not to slip and fall, she stepped gingerly, stabbing the ground with her stout walking stick.

By the time she started back on her second trip, flakes big as bird feathers were blowing. The cold nipped her nose and made it drip. Her forehead ached as she baffled with wind. And she thought wistfully of summertime and the roses blooming there in the crook of her old rail fence.

But she was thankful for her hearty fire and her good dinner on cooking. "When hit's right cold and snowy," she told me, "I'd ruther have me a pot of leather britches and a big onion-head as anything I know. Leather britches air green beans dried. You spread 'em out in the sun, or string 'em up, and they dry and git hard. When yo're ready to cook 'em, you wash 'em and parebile 'em, and that swells 'em all up. With a smidgen of fatback fer seasonin' —I tell you, there hain't no better eatin'. And hit sticks to the ribs."

During the afternoon the storm's intensity varied from periods of relative calm to the wild onslaught of driven snow. Aunt Titia kept busy. She fed the fire and worked close to its genial blaze. For a time she sewed quilt pieces. Then, to sorta rest her eyes, she took up her knitting.

It was at such moments that memories surfaced. "I jest let my thoughts squander," she said. "I could see Pappy acrost the hearth plain as anything. Like a-many a time, I seed him a-settin' in his cheer, readin' his Bible and a-follerin' the words with his stub finger. Pappy lost two fingers to the knuckle in a bar fight onct.

"And I see Mammy there. Like common she had the cyards on her lap and a big basket of wool aside her. Mammy allus minded cyardin'. Hit give her sich a misery in her shoulders. But she didn't never shirk..."

Aunt Titia's thought drifted back. Absently she twisted her worn gold signet ring. Then she cleared her throat and resumed—"If'n I let my eyes roam the room, seem like fust one and than another'n was a-standin' there. Me old house has seed a lot of life. Times back yonder, they'as allus babies to tend and young uns to teach, and old people a-needin' keer and comp'ny."

That day she had to make do with the cat. Becky was curled up on a chair with her back to the fire. About all she did was yawn, stretch up tall, turn around twice and settle down, folding herself together.

The deep silence everywhere made Aunt Titia feel kind of lonesome. All sounds were muffled by the snowfall till the house seemed like it was swathed in wool. So she got down her old box of pictures.

"When I come acrost Em's pitcher hit putt me in mind of another time hit come a big snow. That day I says to her, 'What you say to wadin' the snow?'

"She says, 'I'm with ye.'

"So we got out yonder in the field. Then, hit'as jest grubbed out and the bresh piled up. Fer devilmint I says, 'You git on that side of this pile and I'll git on this'n, and mebbe we can skeer up a rabbit.'

"So she got on her side and I give hit a lick, and out jumped a rabbit. She says, 'Here hit is!'

"Hit jest stuck there in the snow and couldn't run. We killed hit. And afore we come in, we'd killed five or six rabbits. And *hit a Sunday evenin'*. Pappy says, 'I've a mind to whup you both!'

"Eh, law. Winters hain't now like they was when I'as a-growin' up. Them days the ground froze in the fall and hit stayed froze all winter. And one snow warn't gone afore they'as another'n fell on top of hit." A moment of reflection, then she added—

"And they hain't as many stars as they uster be, nuther. We uster find the Seven Stars—they'as all bunched together, and the Two Lost Twins, and Job's Coffin. But they hain't as many stars as they uster be."

Then, that day going to put away her keepsake box she fell!

"I'as a-scuffin' around in an old par of shoes," she said ruefully, "and the sole was loose. Hit tripped me up."

That was scary. I said, "I hope you weren't hurt."

Somebody rattling by on the road waved to us. Aunt Titia peered after the car, uncertain who it was, but responded with a feeble flutter of her fingers. She dragged her thoughts back. "No'm," she said. "I warn't hurt. the Lord'as with me. Fer I grabbed aholt of the bedkivers. But hit'as a pyore meeracle I didn't fall all over the floor and bust myself wide open."

As it was, only her picture hoard got scattered.

At dusk the smother closed in. The familiar scene beyond her door became so fogged that she could barely make out her woods across the road. An unearthly stillness was broken only by the faint rustle of snowflakes thickly falling. Nobody had gone the road that day, and now, she thought, nobody was likely to.

But before black dark, somebody hollered the house.

"I opened the door," she said, "and I seed a man-pusson a-standin' by the doorstones. Hit'as my cousin, Jonny Lindsay. I says, 'Howdy, Jonny, come in and set a spell.'

"He jest stayed where he was, and the snow kep' a-dustin' down. He says, 'I come to make a bargain with ye, Tish.'

"I says, 'Well, I allus like bargains—if'n I can git the best of 'em.'

"He says, 'You may not git he best of this'n.'

"I says, 'Well, tell me about hit.'

"He says, 'I want to come over here and stay with you. I want to die in this old house.' He says, 'You can have whatever I've got.'

"I says, 'I don't want what you've got Jonny. But the door's open. Yo're welcome. And that hain't from the teeth out.'"

While Uncle Jonny went to bed down his nag (the night before, old Shep had died), Aunt Titia freshened the coffee pot and moved the leather britches onto the blaze, and made up biscuit.

Next morning the snowfall had abated, leaving thirteen inches on the ground. The wind blew, bitter cold and strong, piling up deep drifts till the road was blocked, going and coming.

Aunt Lizzie William's cabin, Whittemore Branch

Chapter XXIV

The winter for them together was cozy. Their companionable sharing of the fireside banished loneliness for two old people. They ate and slept well. She knitted for him wool socks of her own homespun yarn; he carved her out a new dough bowl. They talked aplenty. Uncle Jonny liked to play the banjo, and Aunt Titia ventured to sing. So they pleasured one another a heap.

Soon after his ninety-first birthday, which befell in January, Uncle Jonny cut a tooth. Aunt Titia found this vastly amusing—

"One day he says, 'I believe I'm a-cuttin' a tooth.'

"I says, 'Oh, I don't think so, Jonny.'

"He put his finger in his mouth and says, 'Yes, I am.'

"I says, 'Hit's jest a hard place in yore gum.'

"He says, 'No, hit's got a sharp pint.'

"Two, three days later he says, 'Well, my leetle tooth's come through.'

"I jest laughed and laughed. 'The Bible says, onct a man and twict a child,' I says to him. 'That's you.'

"Hit stayed in his mouth about three month. Then hit got loose and he picked hit out. Hit'as jest narr' and pinted, and the roots warn't all sprangled out, but jest squar'."

Uncle Jonny laid some fence. He cut wood and fetched the water. Aunt Titia commented dryly that Carolina had made a right good man about the house out of him. As soon as the weather mildened for planting time, he hitched up old Jen and turned the garden. John Trail with his mule shared work in the corn field. For Uncle Jonny was mighty particular about Jen. He never worked her hard, but only just enough to keep her fit. She wasn't young anymore.

"Jonny's plumb foolish about that nag of his'n," Aunt Titia averred. "When he come over here he says to me, 'Jen's all the fam'ly I got left.'"

Her health and spirits the best in late years, Aunt Titia was ready for all the springtime's activities. And she was gladdened by the early arrival of the Cornplanter. "I'd ruther to hear him as ary other bird," she told me. "When he comes in the spring, hit's time to plant corn. He's a big bird with some blue on his front. He sings so purty durin' the first and second hoein'. Let hit come a shower of rain and the temper git right thick, he'll set up in the tree and jest make hit ring."

But during corn planting, tragedy struck. Melissie's young husband was killed in a fight over twenty-five cents. He happened into Pink Meader's store just as two loafers got into an argument over a shiny new quarter. One pulled a gun, the other leapt at him, and in the scuffle they crashed into the potbelly stove. Will Mears was shot through the heart.

And worse yet for Aunt Titia, less than a month later Melissie died in an automobile accident. Ironically, of five young people riding together, she was the only one injured.

Tillie told me, "It was pore Uncle Jonny had to break the news to her granny. He come a-drivin' home in the moonshine. He said slow as Old Jen was, she went too fast. Every step, he thought he jest couldn't go on. It took all his courage to face Aunt Tish that night."

Their solace was Melissie's little boy Neddy who came to stay awhile with the old folks.

That visit seemed ideal to Tillie—"Uncle Jonny has that youngun in his pocket half the time," she said happily. "He carries him around and takes him places. If he sits, he's a-trottin' the little feller on his knee. He couldn't be more proud if Neddy was his very own son. I reckon when him and Aunt Caroline had all them girls, they was always kindly hopin' fer at least one boy."

I first saw them together early on a June morning, heading for the cornfield. Uncle Jonny, hoe over his shoulder, strode ahead. Close behind him trudged the small boy in patched overalls and ragged straw hat, a hoe just his size over his shoulder.

Aunt Titia's eyes followed them. "Younguns mought as well larn," she said. "They won't allus be somebody to shake the pots and the hoe han'le." She turned back into the house. "My old pappy allus said he'd larn us to work whuther he larnt us to love hit or not. 'If'n you don't have to work,' he uster say, 'Hit won't hurt ye to fergit hit. But hit ud come hard to larn.'"

And so they taught Neddy to be proud of sharing their labors. He had his own little basket to fill with chips at the woodpile, and his special bucket for fetching water from the spring. Sitting on the edge of the porch with his feet dangling, he carefully washed the ground from fresh dug potatoes, laying them in a neat row beside him. And when Aunt Titia baked a cake, he had to help, breaking the eggs. He was a busy and obedient little chap.

"He'd a-better to mind," Aunt Titia said. "I tell you, if'n some of these younguns about fryin'-size age was mine, I'd whup 'em if'n I had to sew 'em up in a bedsheet. Times hain't now like they was back yonder. When we'as a-growin' up, childern had to mind their payrents. Nowadays, the payrents has to mind the childern. And the childern don't keer no more fer their payrents than you would fer a dog you'd whupped off'n a sheep."

As the boy's sixth birthday approached, Uncle Jonny went out in the woods and got runners to make a little sled just like the big one old Jen pulled about. Man and boy set to work under a shadebush in back of the house, the one creating, the other intently watching.

As Uncle Jonny trimmed and fitted, a bumblebee winged in between his face and his hands to enter a crevice among fallen leaves on the earth bank nearby. Pretty soon the bee emerged and flew off, right under Uncle Jonny's nose. Old grandsir glanced quizzically over his silver-rimmed spectacles. The youngster's eyes sparkled and his cheeks dimpled. After a bit, the bee or his twin came home again and disappeared between the leaves. Presently he reappeared and took off once more.

So Uncle Jonny thought up a little game. Picking up a twig, he broke it into short lengths. "What you say we keep track of how many trips Mr. Bee makes?"

Neddy approved with a nod so vigorous it nearly upset him from his seat on a log.

"You take these now," Uncle Jonny instructed him, "and ever' time he flies off, you putt a leetle stick in yore hat."

Through nearly an hour the bee came and went undisturbed by their presence. And by the time the sled was finished, sticks in the little straw hat tallied fourteen journeys near and far.

Aunt Titia and I were on hand to watch Neddy's first ride. John Trail had stopped by. And old Jen down in the field, seeing us clustered near the stable, ambled up the hill to stand with her head drooping in our circle.

At once the sled became Neddy's favorite plaything. Not content with pulling it about during the day, he wanted to take it to bed with him. Forbidden that, he insisted on finding it in plain sight when he opened his eyes each morning. Aunt Titia fashioned for him a "baby brother", near life size, out of corn shucks and rags to ride in the sled when he wasn't dragging vegetables from the garden.

It was a joyful summer the old folks spent keeping their youngster occupied and entertained. Uncle Jonny made him a gourd fiddle. Aunt Titia tied a string to the leg of a big iridescent green and bronze beetle so the child could let it fly and hear it buzz. Neddy's preoccupation was intense, watching it crawl over his bare knee, murmuring in a small voice, "Pretty bug? Pretty bug?"

His uncle gave him a little pig. "He takes hit out with a rope on hit's hind foot," Aunt Titia told me, turning a fond glance toward the boy absorbed at play with his make-believe brother. "He'll set and watch hit eat. Then he comes a-drivin' hit in with his leetle hick'ry."

She and Uncle Jonny patiently helped him learn his part in a play given at the church. Neddy was supposed to be an old man. The program would be long remembered. Aunt Titia was delighted. "He jest stood up there, folded his hands behind his back, and told his piece from start to finish." Everybody admired Neddy. And he was so proud.

But come fall, they had to give up their tadpole of a boy. Along with some of his cousins he would be starting to school. Alone again, the old folks sadly missed him.

That year I left Laurel Fork never dreaming that I'd not soon return.

Aunt Titia was by herself the evening I stopped for farewells. But she was expecting Uncle Jonny momently. She had been reading—"I read the Bible through last winter," she said, with a slight gesture toward the good book left open under the lamp, its faded ribbon-marker limp across the page. "And now I've started agin. I cain't remember nothin'; so hit's like a new book each time."

Her failing memory she accepted cheerfully. *That* she could spare more readily than strength of body. And she rejoiced that now she felt quite peart. "The Bible says, them that waits on the Lord'll renew their stren'th," she quoted. "They'll run and not be weary. They'll walk and not faint. And," she finished with her crinkly smile, "seem like hit's so."

That night when she lighted me off the porch, I could leave without concern for her safety. Uncle Jonny would soon be there.

From the margin of the woods I looked back. A round moon climbed the cloudless sky. Downside the hill, beyond the snake-rail fence and grassy slope, loomed her little hut, black-shadowed in the moonlight that silvered the shakes and glossed the quiet leaves round about. Dim lamplight yellowed her small crooked window beside the chimney. Pale wood smoke vapored upward, scenting the still crisp air. The night was alive with the unceasing chorus of shrill insect voices. Coming up the hill old Jen appeared, bearing Uncle Jonny home.

Chapter XXV

A dozen years passed before I could return to my friends of the Laurel Fork. Though a few letters passed between us at first, as my absence was prolonged and distances increased, our correspondence eventually ceased.

After so long, I hardly knew what to expect when I called at Tillie's door one cold March morning. But time had not changed her, nor the warmth of her greeting. Her eyes lit up, she laughed her deep throaty chuckle and held out her arms. Her welcome just enfolded me.

I had interrupted her cutting out identical print dresses for her twin girls; it made no difference, everything was left lay. She couldn't wait to pull chairs before the fire for a real visit. She had good news of her own large family. But, sadly, the old folks were both gone now.

"Uncle Jonny done his last work the summer he was a hundred year old," she told me. "Not because his stren'th failed, but his judgment, you might say.

"He was still mighty peart fer work. Like when the orchard grass was ripe—you know how scythin' it, you git that sweet smell. When Uncle Jonny come to the house fer dinner, he hung his hat on the wall, and he says to Aunt Tish, 'I can cut orchard grass half a day and come in and eat more'n three men ought.'

"Them two never knowed the meanin' of the word idleness. Every year they put in the garden and their patch of corn. They kep' up with the hoein' and fodder pullin'. They took a sight of satisfaction in the old homeplace. And in each other.

"When Uncle Jonny blowed out them one hundred little white candles on his birthday cake, he says, 'The day I was ninety year old, I mind sayin' then—I've reached old age pint-blank to enjoy hit. And, folks, let me tell ye, *I have.*'

"The old gent surely to goodness looked it," she added fondly, "he was that upright and lively."

From the back of her Bible she took a newspaper clipping that described Uncle Jonny's birthday celebration. While I perused it, she hurried off to the spring so that we might enjoy a fresh drink.

Happy and merry as a schoolboy (it read), Uncle Jonathan Lindsay celebrated his one hundredth birthday with a bountiful anniversary dinner and religious services at his home on Laurel Fork. With two strong puffs the old gentleman blew out the 100 candles on his huge birtyhday cake and challenged younger quests to test their lung power with him.

In spite of his one hundred years, Uncle Jonny's memory is bright and unimpaired. He can write a plain legible hand, tell a good story, and walk where he wishes as comfortably as many men much younger.

After dinner a shooting match was held in which the spry centenarian took part. With one of his grandsons to act as gun rest for him, he shot accurately, his eye true and his aim straight.

When asked to what he attributed his long life, the grand old man replied, "Hard work, common sense, self-control, simple habits and faith in the wisdom of the Lord."

He said he was glad to round out his hundred years in the mountains where he was born and where life is good.

A host of Uncle Jonny's relatives and friends dropped in, many of them coming from great distances, and the day was spent in feasting and visiting and story telling.

Thumbing through memories, reaching back beyond the tumultuous years of the War Between the States, Uncle Jonny recalled when the Indians stayed overnight in his father's house. They slept on the floor before the fire. The squaws carried all the rations and blankets; the bucks carried only their bows and arrows. "Those Indians were not bad people to have around," Uncle Jonny said. They never stole and they never talked. Only their spokesman replied to questioning.

Uncle Jonny enlisted in the Confederate army at the beginning of hostilities and went through the war without a scratch. After the surrender, he returned home bringing with him his gun, which he has used all his life, and a wooden box in which he stored his keepsakes—family letters and photographs, his discharge from the army, and a worn testament which he carried all through his term of service and which he held in his hand when he had his picture taken to leave with his family. "All the fellers had to have some kind of weapon," Uncle Jonny said. "But I says, 'I'm a-goin' to hold this good book over my heart.'"

In the evenin' of his life the old gentleman has read the New Testament twenty-five times. And there is a neatly kept tally on the flyleaf of his Bible.

His years have been filled with labor, adventure, some joys and keen disappointments, but mostly he has found contentment.

"People don't enjoy life half as much today, not half as much, as they did when I was a boy." he said. "They have too much and want too much more. They're never satisfied."

"Men were strong, but gentle and humane, back then," he said. "There wasn't the fighting and shooting and murdering there is today. When liquor was made, trouble started."

Uncle Jonny keeps liquor on hand only for medicinal purposes. He said, "I never had no hankering for any kind of liquor, except sober liquors such as coffee and herb teas."

His years rest lightly on him. But the old gentleman objected to pictures. "They make me look 200 years old," he said. "Pictures show too many wrinkles. I'm only 100. Feel my muscle."

Dancing was a favorite pastime of Mr. Lindsay's youth. "And we really danced in those days," he said. "None of this mincy gliding and skipping. We covered the floor, with plenty of action."

In his heart still smolders the fires of youth. Uncle Jonny did what he called "a little three-legged dancing." While one of his grandsons played the fiddle, the old gentleman cut a few fancy capers, clogging and stomping his cane. His remarkable wife, Aunt Titia, herself now ninety-six, looked on smiling.

"Fer all his gladness in the day," Tillie continued, dippering me a fresh cold drink, "Uncle Jonny didn't forget his nag. He took old Jen out a piece of his birthday cake. You know what a sweet tooth she had, and he always pampered her.

"Jen hadn't been so peart since late in the last spring. But then she was old as Methusly, fer a horse. Uncle Jonny said she was jest naturally slowin' down like ever'body else a-growin' old, and deserved a rest. He said she'd been a good and faithful worker all her life long, and he wanted to make her comfortable.

"About five weeks after his birthday, there come a spell of snow and real cold weather. Jen was off her feed. With no teeth much, she had to have special rations.

"One evenin' Uncle Jonny trudged his way out to the stable to look after Jen. And he never got back. Look like he misjudged the path and fell down in a big drift that was too deep fer him to get up. And he lay dead when Aunt Tish found him. From the snow-sleep, they figgered.

"Old Jen soon follered him. And Aunt Tish too. She jest wasn't herself no more. She took it awful hard. John he come over to stay with her in the old house. She fixed the meals and worked on her quilts. But you could tell, her heart wasn't in it. She looked so wizened and woebegone, and dreary as sin in her black dress and headrag. She even folded away her woven coverlids she had put on the beds. The old house was a picture fer Uncle Jonny's birthday celebration.

"It just broke my heart to see Aunt Tish so grievin'. She missed Uncle Jonny so. She says to me, 'His hat looks mighty forlorn a-hangin' there on the wall.'

"And up on the shelf alongside the clock was a jar of peaches Uncle Jonny helped her can. Said she was keepin' 'em fer a memorial to him.

"Well, Aunt Tish just pined and pindled. I recollect she told me onct, 'Some nights I go to bed and I git to travelin'. I see ever' body I ever knowed.'"

Sadly Tillie concluded, "I reckon it happened one of those times, and the dear old soul just naturally kep' on a-travelin'. For come mornin', she never woke up. She was ninety-five years, eight months and twenty-four days old."

Not quite the century she had in mind, but near enough when a body no longer cares, one way or the other.

Aunt Titia's last words to me were, "Well, come back and see me—if'n I hain't a-livin', why you can see the place whur they putt me."

She lay high on the slope of the old burial ground facing the Locust Knob schoolhouse. The small gravestone bore only her name and dates: Letitia Trail, July 23, 1845 - April 17, 1941. But appropriate to it would have been the words of her favorite hymn, the swinging "Beulah Land":

> "As on the highest mount I stand,
> I look away across the sea
> Where mansions are prepared for me..."

Happily it were so. For her humble earthy dwelling was no more. The highway builders, slashing through her solitary woods, had straightened the curve of the road. A ribbon of paving covered the spot where her cabin once stood, and her lordly oak tree. No vestige of her small world remained. But as she once said, "Our friends don't never leave out—onless we fergit 'em."

And Aunt Titia is unforgetable.

Trail cabin by moonlight

Toxaway family

Banks family, Whittemore Branch

Eilleen Gardner Galer
Author/Photographer

Eilleen Galer was born in Charlotte, North Carolina in 1906. She traveled throughout the mountains of North Carolina as a young writer observing and recording the dialect and way of life of the Appalachian Mountain people whose lifestyle has long disappeared. At 90 she feels obliged to write about these fine people to preserve their heritage for all to appreciate.

Eileen Galer is a freelance writer and has been a photographer for over 70 years, specializing in the preservation of animals and vanishing scenes and lifestyles. She was an officer for 20 years in the National Photographic Society in Washington, DC, and received the NPS Shaw Memorial Trophy for outstanding service in 1961. Her work is in the permanent collection of the National Photographic Society of America. Ms. Galer developed and presented a humane education outreach program for the Arlington Animal Welfare League, which included a photo essay designed to promote kindness to animals. This program has been viewed by more than 10,000 people of all ages.

Eileen Galer recently authored a biography titled *Eugen Weisz, Painter—Teacher*, and a photographic book *God Barking in Church: And Further Glimpses of Animal Welfare*, both currently in bookstores. She also has contributed to two editions of the photographic book series *American Photographers at the Turn of the Century*, also available in bookstores. She has contributed to *Cats* magazine, *Cat Fancy*, *Advocate* (American Humane Association) and the *Journal of the Photographic Society of America*. She has been a *National Finalist* in the *Washington Star* animal category, *First* for farm animals by the American Humane Association, and won the *First Place Cup* for monochrome prints and color slides and *Print of the Year* by the National Photographic Society, Washington, DC.

Eileen Galer's love for life reverberates throughout these pages. Her sparkling wit and charming style enliven her stories enabling future generations to know, appreciate, and cherish past lifestyles and events.

Additional titles showcasing the work of Eilleen Gardner Galer:

Eugen Weisz: Painter—Teacher

God Barking in Church
And further Glimpses of Animal Welfare

The Art of the Human Form

American Photographers at the Turn of the Century
Nature & Landscapes

American Photographers at the Turn of the Century
Travel & Trekking

Just Folks - Here and There

Available from Five Corners Publications